Page 134, paragraph two,
should read:

Shuttle 'Challenger' in 1986...

Other Books by the Same Authors

By Ben Partridge and Cora Cheney:

Alfred A. Knopf, New York:

China Sea Roundup

Rendezvous In Singapore

Coward-McCann, New York:

Underseas: The Challenge Of The Deep Frontier

Dodd, Mead, New York:

Crown Of The World: A View Of The Inner Arctic

By Cora Cheney:

Holt, Rinehart, and Winston, New York:

Skeleton Cave

Fortune Hill

Rumpus On Commodore Hill

The Rocking Chair Buck

The Christmas Tree Hessian

Plantation Doll

Key Of Gold

Alfred'A. Knopf, New York:

The Doll Of Lilac Valley

The Peg Legged Pirate Of Sulu

The Mystery Of The Disappearing Cars

The Girl At Jungle's Edge

Hawthorn, New York:

The Treasures Of Lin Li-Ti

Scribners, New York:

The Incredible Deborah

Dodd, Mead, New York:

The Case Of The Iceland Dogs

Tales From A Taiwan Kitchen

Alaska: Indians, Eskimos, Russians And The Rest

Stephen Greene Press, Brattleboro, VT.:

Vermont, The State With The Storybook Past

Countryman Press, Taftsville, VT,:

Profiles From The Past

Florida's Family Album
A History for All Ages

By Cora Cheney and Ben Partridge

San Marcos Press
St. Marks, Florida

Published by the San Marcos Press
P.O. Box 276, St. Marks, Florida 32355

ISBN O-9636651-0-3

Printed in the United States of America, May 1993
First Printing

Designed by Moses Rodin,Gallery Graphics, Tallahassee, FL.
Printed by Rose Printing Co., Tallahassee, FL.
Print: 12/10 Bookman
Style: The Chicago Manual of Style, 13th Ed.

Illustration Credits: Black and white:
Florida Bureau of Archaeological Research, p.7, Frank Gilson; p.24.
Florida State Archives,
pp.5,14,16,19,22,27,28,38,43,49,53,55,56,58,59,60.63,66,79,81,82,84,86,
87,89,91,93,94,100,105,107,108,109,112,113,115,120,122,124,125,126,127,
131,133,137,138,147,155,157,159,161.
All others and all maps, Ben Partridge.
Color section:
Ben Partridge, Saber tooth cat or tiger, Fla. citrus gold.
St. Petersburg Times, Miami-FSU football, Miami Beach, Hurricane Andrew.
Florida A & M Univ. University Relations, Keith Pope, FAMU Marching 100 Band.
Florida State Univ., Dance Dept. Jon Nalon, Dancers.
Florida Dept. of Commerce, Division of Tourism, Skyway Bridge, Sport
Fishing, Capitol Complex, Modern Seminoles
Cover: Photo By Ben Partridge, at the De Soto National Memorial, National
Park Service, Bradenton, FL.

Price: $14.95

Distributed by BookWorld Services, Inc.,
1933 Whitfield Park Loop, Sarasota, FL 34243

Order Toll-Free 800/444-2524

*For our grandchildren:
Ben, Cheney, Mathias,
Nicholas, Rose, Tatiana,
and Tyler.*

Preface

Having retired from careers in the military, lawyering, teaching, travelling, preaching, and parenting, two old history buff writers who sit on their front porch overlooking the St.Marks and Wakulla Rivers naturally dream of writing a history of Florida for posterity. So we did.

We could not have done it without the help of the State Library of Florida, especially Mary Ann Cleveland, librarian of the Florida Collection. We are grateful to Joan Morris, curator of the Florida State Archives, and the assistant curator Joanna Norman who provided us with a treasure trove of old photographs.

Dixie Nims, photo-librarian of the Florida Department of Tourism generously supplied us with dazzling color photographs of the contemporary state. We are also beholden to Andrew Barnes for making available the photographic archives of the *St. Petersburg Times*. Special thanks go also to Keith Pope of the FAMU Public Relations office and to the Dance Department of FSU who both provided color illustrations.

Staff persons at the Florida Bureau of Archaeological Research and Ed Lane of the Florida Bureau of Geology made special materials available, which have proved most valuable.

We especially appreciate the work of those experts whose comments appear on the first page for reading the manuscript in rough draft.

Family Bibles, old kinfolk lore, and being on the Florida scene for many decades gave us a scenario for a story that is more of a family saga than an account of the glitter and glitz of the gold coast. Florida is bound by the heroes and heroines who make the framework for a readable history.

Cora Cheney and Ben Partridge

Table of Contents

To the Reader

You might go walking in Florida and find the bones of a rhinoceros! Of course there are none of these animals living in the wild in Florida today, but there once were. It might make you think you had accidentally stepped into Africa. In a sense, maybe you did, for it is believed that Florida was once part of Africa.

The first chapter of this book sets the stage for the exotic and unique land of Florida, the twenty-seventh state, with a history often so bizarre, violent, and stormy that the true story should be told.

Can you find your place in this family history?

Chapter One

Florida Prehistory

In the Beginning

Can you believe that Florida was once covered by chilly seas? We have evidence of this because in the phosphate mines at Mulberry in 1988 the whole skeleton of a twenty-five foot baleen whale was discovered. Baleen whales only survive in colder waters where there is plankton, which includes "krill", small sea creatures similar to shrimp, on which they can feed.

That whale must have found many such tiny creatures in the then cold Florida sea. Baleen whales are also called whalebone whales because old fashioned ladies and girls often wore whalebone corsets which were made from the mouth structure of these ocean creatures.

Of course, there was no land here when that whale appeared. How did Florida happen, how did it get its land, vegetation, animals, and finally the people?

Religious and scientific theories sometimes disagree about the details of the creation of the world, and the scientists who work to solve the mysteries of the far past may disagree with each other as new theories develop.

Some of the major sciences we now rely upon to tell us our past are geology, the study of the physical history of the earth and the rocks and minerals that compose it; archaeology, the study of people and their artifacts, the things they made and used; and anthropology, the study of the origins of people, their social and cultural development and beliefs.

Geologists believe that Florida is one of the youngest parts of the United States, and that it is a growing rock platform now surrounded on three sides by the sea. This rock platform has built up over many years on a foundation of igneous rocks formed within the earth's molten center now referred to as our "basement". The Florida peninsula has probably been growing and developing into its present shape for the last 200 to 300 million years with the south tip having been gradually completed from six million to 100 thousand years ago.

The world is composed of plates, and the study of plate movement is called "plate tectonics". If you tried to make a paper globe you would start with flat pieces of paper and paste them together cleverly so you would end up with a round shape with a series of flat segments or plates. Imagine that some of the flat paper segments slipped and changed positions. This may well be what happened during the early history of our world. The plates of the world, having cooled into solid sheets, could then shift or roll on the hot molten liquid in the center of the earth. Plates did apparently shift from place to place, occasionally colliding with each other and causing either a mountain range if the edges tilted upward or a great trough or depression if the edges tilted downward.

There is a growing theory that the early world of many millions of years ago was at one time made up of a super-continent composed of what is now North and South America, Africa, Europe and other lands. This body split up, then was forced back together to form another unit which geologists call "Pangea" which also finally split apart. Recent research indicates that the area we now call Florida was probably once a part of Northwestern Africa. There is much evidence to support such a theory.

Florida's basic geology differs somewhat from the geology of the United States north of us but appears more likely to resemble the geology of Africa. Animal remains in the phosphate mines include the fossils of early camels and rhinoceros, animals not found in the

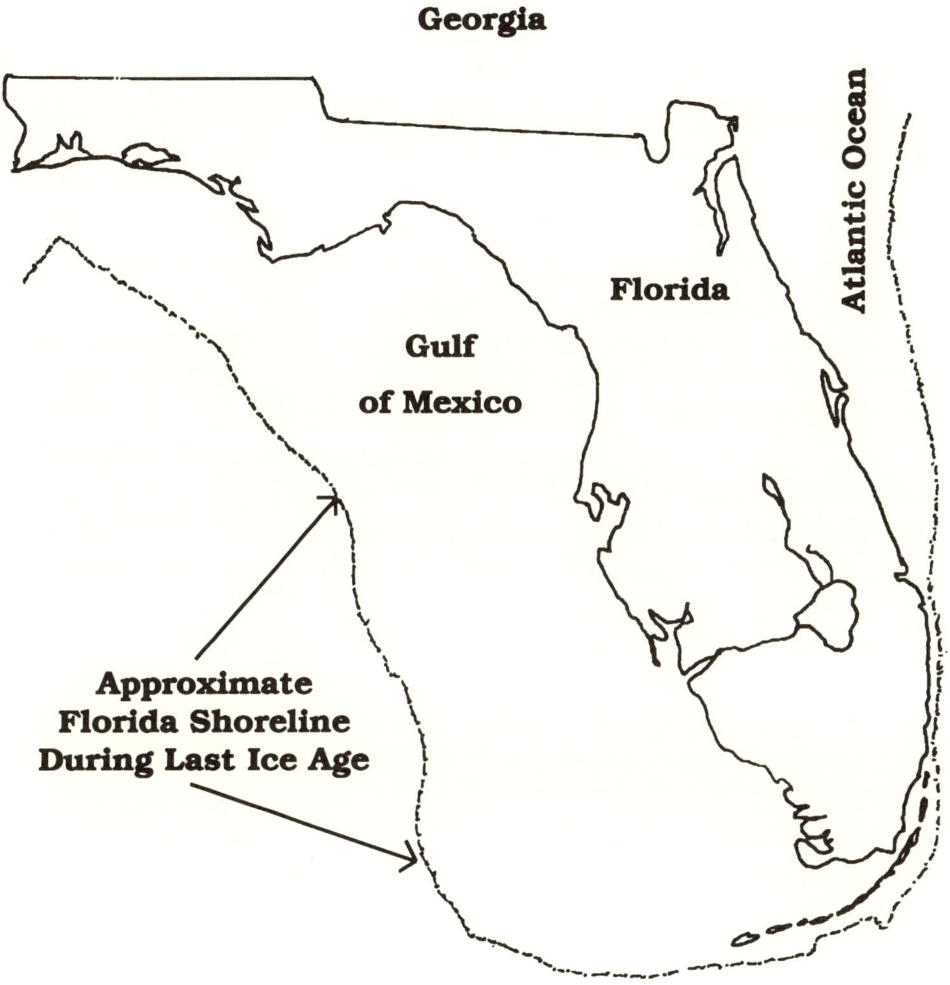

Georgia
Atlantic Ocean
Florida
Gulf
of Mexico
Approximate
Florida Shoreline
During Last Ice Age

United States but in Africa. There appears to be a geological line in south Georgia, just above the present Florida state line which geologists call a "suture" line where Florida could, many years ago, have been pushed against and joined to what is now Georgia. Geology is science fiction at its best!

For various reasons which we don't fully understand, the world has long undergone warming and chilling trends. When a substantial part of the world is cold, the water which falls there does so in the form of snow or sleet, with more falling than is melting. This forms the massive sheets of ice called glaciers and causes the sea levels to go down for lack of new water When these parts of the world then turn warmer, the glaciers melt and run into the seas, causing the sea levels to rise.

In early times, when the glaciers contained more water and the sea was lower, Florida's land mass became higher with more dry land exposed and the coastline located farther out. Water was scarcer for humans and animals during these glacial periods. The changing sea levels, by wave action on the beaches during these periods, created terracing which is still apparent in the Florida we know today.

We know that, during the last glacial period, about 10,000 to 15,000 years ago, while the sea levels were low and much more of Florida was dry land, ancient humans lived and hunted animals in areas which are now sea bottom. A daring new breed of archaeologists recently put on divers' suits and entered the sea around Florida to study the remains of animals and the artifacts made by the people who lived there when this was dry land.

In the sea bottom, they have found old streams and springs. Some fresh water springs still flow into the salt water that now covers these areas. Both the animals and the people who hunted them frequented the areas where fresh water was found at this early period of history.

The numerous old fresh water rivers that still flow into the sea are storehouses of historical material. In

Discovering a mastadon in Wakulla Spings, 1957

1981 divers in the lower Wacissa River in Jefferson County found the skull of an ancient bison with a chert weapon point inbedded in it. In 1982 this find was sampled and photo documented by diver/archaeologist James Dunbar of the Florida Bureau of Archaeological Research. The small weapon point is not believed to have killed this large animal, but spear thrusts were likely responsible for its death. These bones are believed to be about 11,000 years old. This is a most significant find for scientific detectives, for it shows that the humans and animals lived together at that time in that place. It also shows that humans had constructed weapons with which they were able to kill this massive and dangerous animal.

5

The First Floridians

So who were these people and where did they come from, these ancient humans who appeared on the Florida scene from 15,000 to 10,000 years ago? They were the ancestors of modern Indians, and they came from Asia.

The present sea bottom between the northeastern end of Russian Siberia and the northwestern end of Alaska, the Bering Strait, an area now known as Beringea, was at times during the last glacial period, exposed as dry land when the water fell as snow or ice and built up the glaciers. People and animals could move across this surface, known as the Bering Land Bridge, from Asia to North America.

The first humans and animals to come across during these periodic dry but cold periods were the Caucasoid people we now call Indians. They spread over the new lands of North America, apparently travelling and surviving between the large glaciers of this period, some of them finally reaching the more moderate climate of Florida. Most of the prehistoric people in South America apparently walked through North America to their new homes. The last people to cross the Land Bridge before the sea finally rose and covered it were the Mongoloid people we now know as Eskimos, who moved east and north and did not come to Florida.

We know very little about the prehistoric Floridians and we can only guess at what their new land looked like. We do know that Florida was bigger then than it is now. It was undoubtedly colder and drier but there were enough water and grasses to sustain both human and animal life. The landscape is believed to have been mostly grassy savannahs, with few if any forests.

Remains of animals which likely came across the Land Bridge have been found in Florida sites and include the mammoth, sabertoothed cat or tiger, ancient bison, giant three toed sloth, giant armadillo, mastodon, horse, peccary, and dire wolf. The rhinoceros and camel may

Paleo Hunters

have originated in Africa or Asia during the very early plate tectonic shifts. No evidence has yet been found that Florida was ever the home of the great reptiles, the dinosaurs. Marine fossils found in Florida include shark teeth, rays, whales, and dugong or sea cows, ancestors of our present manatees. Bones of both animals and humans are dated by a process called radioactive carbon dating or carbon-14 dating. The age of organic materials can be fairly accurately estimated by measuring their remaining carbon content.

The very ancient human and animal bones have usually been found around springs, river banks, and sink holes, which are called "cenotes" by archaeologists. Geologically, Florida is principally a "karst" area which usually contains sink holes, caves, springs, disappearing streams, and lakes which periodically drain through sudden holes in their bottoms. Karst areas are created by ground water dissolving limestone.

The mysterious first Indians in Florida were labelled Paleo, meaning ancient. The came on foot, a few at a time, clothed in skins if at all. They hunted from one water source to another and created no large settlements. Their weapons were made of flint or chert, bones, or shells. Sometimes the weapons were attached to wooden shafts or handles. They also used a double weight bolo type throwing device which entangled smaller animals or birds. Later they developed a spear thrower called an "atalatl", a clever hand throwing device which increased the leverage, speed and range for thrown spears.

Around 9,000 or so years ago the climate of Florida had become milder and more humid. This began the period of the Archaic, meaning old, Indians. By this time many of the earlier animals had disappeared so they had to depend more on food gathered from the land, fresh waters, and the sea. Archaeologists find more artifacts and changes in living patterns in this period. The settlements became larger, and later Indians of this period began making some pottery.

Migration Routes During Ice Age

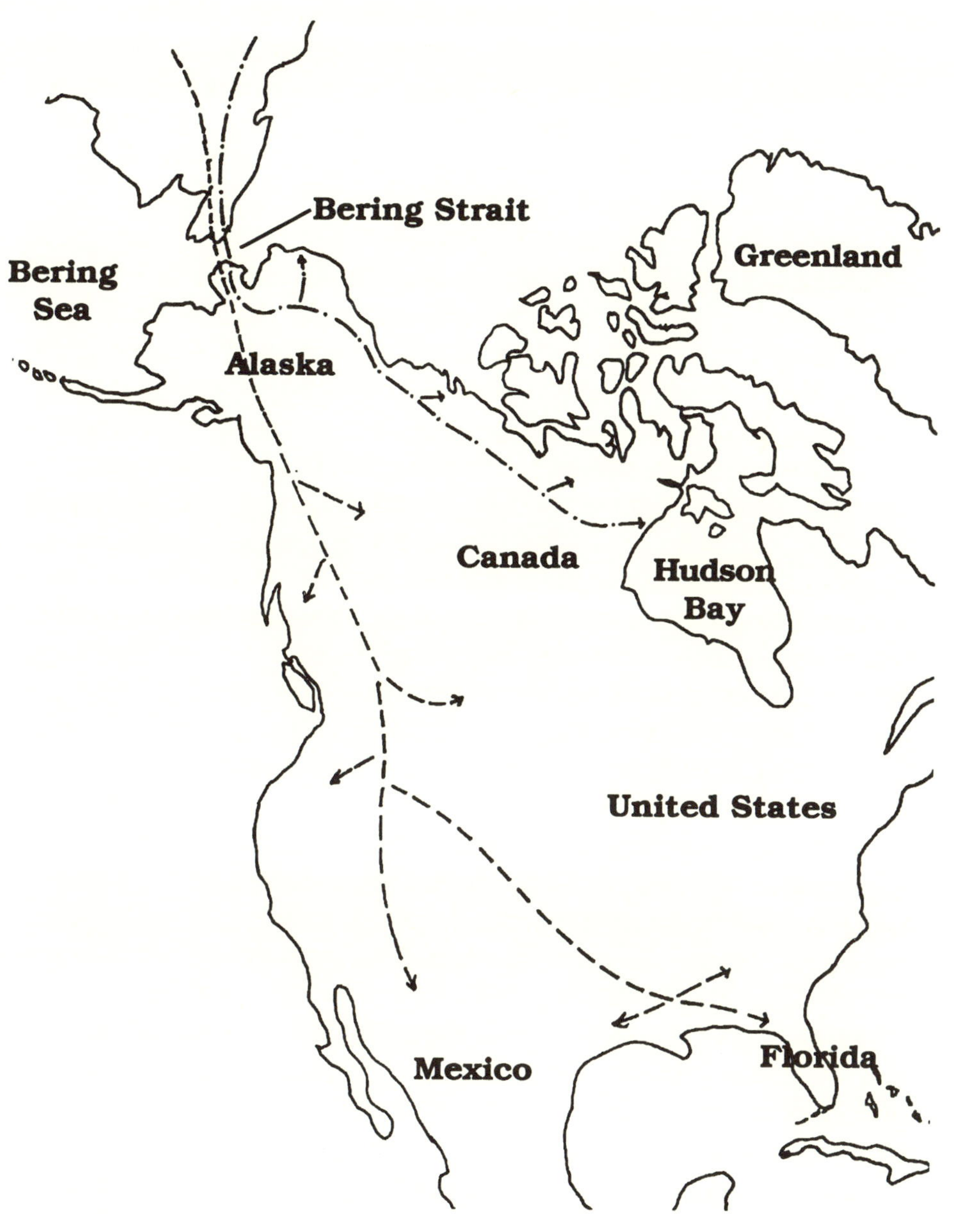

The Woodland Indians, so named because there were forests on some of the land at this period, are the people whose lives we begin to follow about 3,000 years ago. These are the Indians who were in Florida when the Spaniards came in the early 1500's. They became much more advanced, creating ornate pottery and large settlements. They were mound builders, leaving these great memorials for us to admire today.

In or near the towns of Fort Walton, Bradenton, Tallahassee, and many others, Indian mounds rise in the midst of highways and shopping malls. Look for them, they are hard to miss. Unfortunately many irreplaceable mounds have been demolished to make room for houses and highways.

Some of the mounds were burial sites, some were for ceremonial purposes and some were piles of community waste materials, called "middens". Only a prosperous society could build and maintain the mounds, huge man made hills, with soil or shells laborously carried by hand. These man hours would have been used for food gathering or growing in a poorer society.

The mounds were very much part of the Indian culture when the Spanish arrived, for there have been Spanish trade goods found in some mounds along with Indian pottery and artifacts. During this period, Indians had learned to till the soil and raise and store crops, including squash and corn or maize.

There were an estimated 100,000 Indians in Florida when the Spanish arrived. By now the Indians were roughly divided into tribal groups: the Timucuans, the Apalachees, and the Tocobago in the north; to the south the Calusa and Tequesta; and smaller groups called Keys, Jeaga, and Ais.

After contact with the Europeans, the Indians began almost at once to die out from European diseases to which they had no immunity, and from warfare with the Europeans and with other Indians. When the Spanish took over food supplies and wrecked the hunting lands,

LeMoyne sketch of Indians

the Indians starved. Pottery making by the Indians declined for the Indians preferred European trade items. Mound building ceased as the village populations decreased.

For 12,000 to 15,000 years the prehistoric Indians had created a culture including artistic, religious, political and survival skills. After about 200 years of contact with Europeans they were almost totally wiped out, with only a few thousand Indians left in Florida, remnants of their once proud civilization.

These remaining first Indians were, in general, the ancestors of later tribal groups: the Creeks, Chickasaws, Cherokees, Miccosukees, and other smaller groups. The Seminoles, meaning "runaways" were not a tribe in the usual sense. They were remnants of other tribes who had run away from other areas and some escaped slaves who bonded together generally to resist the white intruders. Indian history is complex and heartbreaking, and we will find out more about them as this book develops.

Chapter Two

The Spanish Conquest of Florida 1513-1763

Indian

I don't know who this Indian is,
A bow within his hand,
But he is hiding by a tree
And watching white men land.
They may be gods—they may be fiends—
They certainly look rum.
He wonders who on earth they are
And why on earth they've come.
Rosemary and Stephen Vincent Benet.
A Book of Americans
New York: Rinehart & Co., 1933.

Ponce de Leon

It could have been a little Indian girl, playing under a palm tree on a dune near present day St. Augustine, who first saw the three ships rise over the horizon, moving toward Florida out of the Atlantic Ocean on an April day in 1513.

Of course she ran to tell her mother, who like any Timucuan adult, probably dismissed the crazy story of great white bird ships out on the ocean. But soon the rest of the people knew that men with white faces, wearing heavy shining clothes, were climbing off the big ships and actually approaching their beach in small boats.

Juan Ponce de Leon, often known as the explorer who

Juan Ponce De Leon in Florida

came to Florida seeking the fountain of youth, actually was on a quest for gold, slaves, and glory. With him Juan Ponce brought alcohol, guns, and European diseases which, to give the man credit, he did not know would eventually help wipe out the Timucuan tribe. But that day, while bewildered Indians watched at a cautious distance, Juan Ponce looked around at the fair scene, claimed it all for Spain, and named it La Florida after the Spanish Pascua Florida, the feast of the flowers at Easter time. There were evidently black slaves in his company, possibly the first blacks in North America.

Probably the greatest thing that Juan Ponce brought

was a smattering of literacy. Of course the Indians could not read and write, nor could many people in Spain, but in Ponce's crew were people who could write logs, letters, and accounts of the trip for future Floridians. A few of these documents remain in Spanish archives. With the arrival of the Spanish expedition that day, Florida history of Indians and Europeans had a recorded beginning.

There may have been earlier European expeditions to the area, such as the voyages of Christopher Columbus, who first saw the Caribbean islands in 1492. However Columbus did not touch the Florida peninsula. Juan Ponce, the nobleman from Leon in Spain, was a member of Columbus' second voyage, and he was bitten by the new world fever to explore, colonize, and Christianize.

Ponce's company did not stay long on the beach, nor did they fight the Indians. Rather they proceeded down the Atlantic coast and probably around the keys and north to present Charlotte Harbor. Of course there were no accurate maps and no Spanish names on the various places so we have to make educated guesses on the routes of all the explorers.

However, thanks to those valuable logs and records we know that Ponce de Leon sailed away from Florida in September, became governor of Puerto Rico, and had other adventures before he returned to Florida, this time in 1521. The King of Spain gave him the right to conquer, govern, and colonize. At his landing spot on Tampa Bay, near Port Charlotte, he found the Indians to be highly hostile. Imagine the surprise and anger of the Indians when Ponce de Leon began to read to them in Spanish. Of course they did not understand the language, but soon they found out what it was all about. Ponce de Leon had a prepared document telling the essential information about the Catholic Church. He read it three times. If, by the end of the third reading, the Indians refused to be converted they were to be considered slaves of Spain. This is an incredible sounding story to us in Florida today.

To the further astonishment of the Indians, the Spanish brought priests, missionaries, and 200 colonists of men, women, and children. There were also sheep, horses, and equipment for building.

Nobody made any records of Spanish children and Indian children making contact, but there were surely play, trading, and learning new words. All we know is that children were there.

When the house building began the Spanish were violently attacked by the Indians. The colonists fled to the ships in terror. Ponce de Leon was fatally injured by an arrow, and the first white colony failed, the survivors returning to Cuba and Spain.

Panfilio de Narvaez, 1528

The Adventures of Panfilio de Narvaez

Florida's second major Spanish explorer was red-headed ferocious Panfilio de Narvaez. After Narvaez explored for Spain in Cuba and Mexico, where he lost an eye in a fight, the King of Spain sent him to explore, conquer, Christianize, and colonize Florida.

He set out from Spain with a company of 600 people, soldiers, women, children, and missionary priests. Some of the people lost heart and deserted en route at islands, and two of his ships were lost in storms. The diminished company landed somewhere in the region of Tampa in April 1528.

The astonished and fearful Indians saw the Spanish and ran away, but old "One Eye" lured them back. He had another mandate from the King to read in Spanish, the same proclamation given by Ponce de Leon—be a Christian or be my slaves!

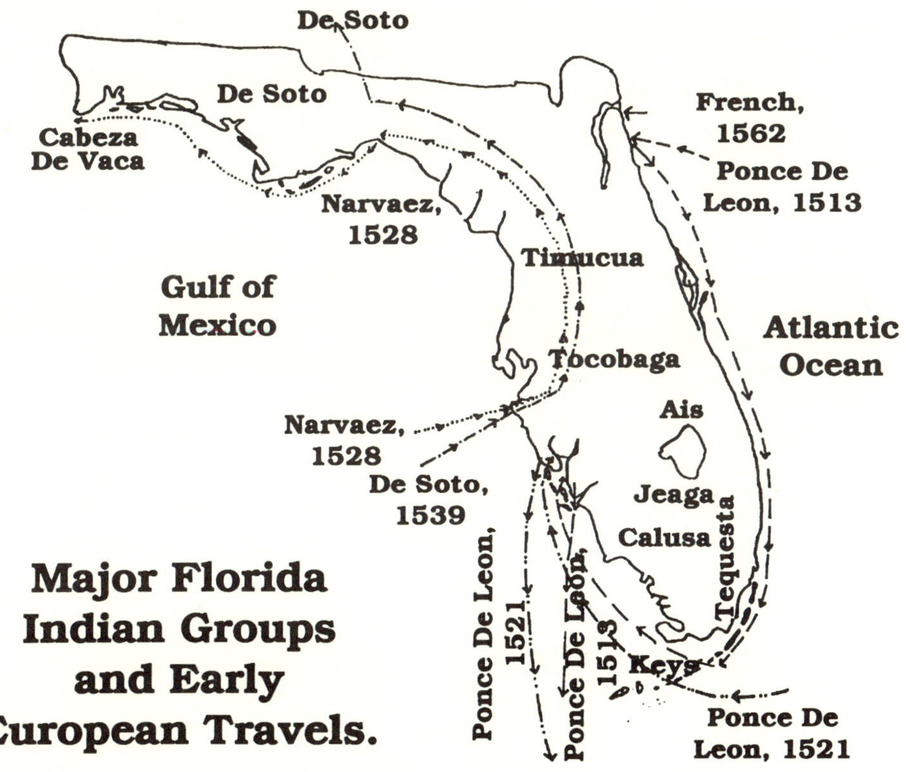

Major Florida Indian Groups and Early European Travels.

Evidently the Indians understood enough by now to respond that they did not want the Spanish there, and the fight broke out.

The Spanish rushed back to their ships where Narvaez made a controversial decision: he wanted to explore the interior of Florida. There were no maps, just fables and faith, but he decided to send the ships north up the Gulf of Mexico, while 300 men and forty horses proceeded north by land. The hope was to meet on some unknown shore. Although the officers and crew were horrified the bizarre plan was put into effect at once.

The women, confined to the ships, blazed out curses and the children shrieked at seeing their fathers depart into the jungle. The soldiers were given rations of two pounds of sea biscuit and a half-pound of bacon.

Hostile Indians, hunger, bugs and no trails to follow made this one of Florida's most horrendous junkets. Two hundred Indians attacked them as they tried to cross the Suwannee River. In June the party reached the estimated area of present day St. Marks, where the Wakulla River and St. Marks River meet near Apalachee Bay.

Predictably, the ships never arrived to meet them. Driven crazy by the biting bugs, sniped at by the Apalachee Indians, half starved and abandoned, they began eating their horses. Then someone had an idea. Tan the horse hides, make bellows of the leather to keep a hot fire going for a forge, melt up armor and swords to make tools and build some ships for escape.

There were now only 250 men left, many of them very ill, but the able ones began to make ships, the first ship building enterprise in North America.

They cut ship timbers from the local trees, used horse tails and palm fibers for ropes and rigging, looked to the pine trees for pitch, resin and tar, and used their clothes for sails. With heroic hard work, by September they had constructed five unseaworthy barges.

They named their port of departure the Bay of Horses and bravely set out for Mexico. Three of the boats carried forty-nine men each and the other two vessels held forty-eight and forty-seven.

Soon the boats began to capsize and most of the people were drowned, including Narvaez. However there were a few who survived and swam to land to begin a long walk west.

Finally, led by Cabeza de Vaca, four people of this remarkable entourage survived outrageous hardships and adventures through the Gulf region, through Texas, finally arriving in Mexico City in 1536, eight years after departing from the Bay of Horses. This was the first recorded foot expedition from coast to coast in American history.

The Long Journey of Cabeza de Vaca

One of the high ranking officers of the original Narvaez expedition was Cabeza de Vaca, an educated man who had violently opposed Narvaez about the inland Florida trek. He thought abandoning the ships in Tampa Bay was the height of folly.(A footnote in history says that the ships with the cursing women and the crying children finally made it back to Spain after failing to make contact with the overland group.)

Cabeza de Vaca wrote the first best selling book

Alvar Nunez Cabeza de Vaca pictured on Spanish postage stamp

about Florida. He recorded this overland journey and the high adventures of the eight years spent getting from Florida to Mexico. He wrote this account as an official report to the King of Spain. First published in 1542 *The Journey of Alvar Nunez Cabeza de Vaca* has been translated into English and is available in scholarly Florida libraries.

Among the four men who completed the journey was North America's first black explorer, Esteban (or Estevan or Estebanita as he is variously called) a Moor from Morocco. Esteban is said to have signed on as a slave, but his wit and courage were of such importance to the survival of the group that he soon was no longer considered a slave.

When the ships were constructed in the St. Marks area Esteban's strength and energy helped keep the

A fanciful sketch of Indians by Jacques LeMoyne

work going. When the ships sank one after the other Esteban was one of the four who survived the eight year hike to Mexico.

One of the many stories of the journey is how de Vaca and Esteban and the other two won the friendship of the Indians by becoming healers, a great change from the Spanish fighters. One of the men was a strongly religious doctor who helped heal an Indian by the laying on of hands. Soon the other two Christians were called upon to also be healers.

Esteban decided to try his skill as a faith healer.

"I'm a Moslem", he said, "but surely I can heal too". He did.

This tale and many other little known bits of Florida related history are recorded in de Vaca's book.

Juan Ortiz

One more legend had its beginning in the Narvaez expedition. Although Narvaez was reportedly cantankerous, stubborn, and at times foolish, his wife loved him. When he failed to return from Florida, she sent a search party under the command of Juan Ortiz to find her husband.

Not only did Ortiz fail to find Narvaez, although he probably heard news of the fate of the party, but he himself was captured by Indians and given up for dead.

In 1539, when Hernando de Soto was again trying to conquer Florida, they found Ortiz near Tampa Bay and rescued him. Ortiz had escaped execution during his captivity through the pleas of the wife and daughter of the Indian chief. The Indian women liked the looks of Ortiz' blue eyes so much that they untied him from the stake just before he was burned to death. Ortiz lived with the Indians until he began to look like one, and he spoke the dialects well. De Soto recognized him by his blue eyes. It was like the better known Pocohontas story which occurred seventy years later in Virginia

De Soto took Ortiz into his exploring party, presumably leaving the Indian maiden behind. Ortiz, with his knowledge of Indians, did much to help de Soto, the third major Spanish explorer, on his wide travels in Florida and North America.

Hernando DeSoto in the Florida wilderness

The Adventures of Hernando de Soto

Hernando de Soto had already explored and looted in South America when at age thirty-six he was ordered by his king to explore Florida, picking up where Ponce de Leon and Narvaez had failed.

Lusting for the gold that the Spanish believed must be hidden in Florida (how could any place so beautiful not have gold too?) he landed in 1539 at Tampa Bay with about 600 troops, priests, women, children, and 300 horses. Like Narvaez he headed overland through the jungles for the Apalachee country of the north. Of course, the Indians, remembering the two previous Spanish explorations and their cruel treatment of the native people, ferociously fought the Spaniards. De Soto enslaved as many Indians as he could.

Many of the troops died on the journey. In October they reached the area of the present Tallahassee where they found an Indian town, Anhaica, with vacant houses and some winter stores of corn, squash, beans and pumpkins. The Spanish moved in, and the Indians who had gone foraging and hunting, were literally out in the cold. De Soto stayed over the winter at this comfortable rent free retreat and when spring came, he set out for further adventures and travels in America.

The Spanish thought all the territory in America was part of Florida and that it all belonged to them. De Soto, by today's mapping, probably led his party into what is now Georgia, Alabama, South Carolina, Tennessee, Mississippi, Texas, Louisiana, and Arkansas. He died in Arkansas, which the Spanish considered Florida, in May 1542, of a fever and was buried in a tributary of the Mississippi River.

The expedition went forward under Luis de Moscosco who was chosen by the dying de Soto and voted on by the soldiers in the best democratic style. He led the survivors to Mexico City with no gold and no permanent settlement left behind. Records of this exploration had lasting value for North America in opening new territory.

Part of this long expedition might be attributed to a wily Apalachee boy who hung around the winter quarters and learned a little Spanish.

"Señor", he said, "I shall share with you a secret. There is great gold in the north. I will lead you to it".

The boy disappeared, back with his own people, but he had told de Soto such a convincing story that the Spanish broke camp and headed out in the spring of 1540, to the delight of the Indians who got back their town of Anhaica.

Archaeologists Calvin Jones (R)
and Richard Vernon at the Desoto site in Tallahassee

24

Discoveries of Archaeologist Calvin Jones

In 1987, about four centuries after de Soto departed the area, a clever archaeologist, Calvin Jones, made a historical discovery near the State Capitol in Tallahassee. He uncovered the winter quarters of Hernando de Soto where his army had camped in 1539.

De Soto's party had left long accounts of the explorations, but nobody knew exactly where they had spent the first winter in Florida. Archaeologists are always watching bulldozers. Calvin Jones, looking at a city construction site, took his own shovel from the trunk of his car and examined the soil, guessing that he might have happened on mission ruins. Jones had spent his Southern boyhood looking for arrowheads and likely Indian spots. This place had an Indian aura about it, but somehow conditions didn't add up to the usual mission site.

Perplexed, he came back the next day and found some odd artifacts, many pieces of rusted chain link. He laid the pieces together. Armor! It was chain mail armor, a kind of metal cloth, worn for protection against Indian arrows when the heavy steel traditional armor was too hot and heavy.

Jones and his helpers decided that this must have been the long sought de Soto winter camp, Anhaica, deserted nearly 450 years ago. The builders agreed to postpone construction while scientists went to work with spades and strainers. While press and television cameras, professional and amateur archaeologists, and curious people looked on, diggers pulled out glass beads, many more iron links, coins, and even the jawbone of a hog, not native to Florida. De Soto was the only known Spanish explorer to have brought along pigs for food, and the carbon testing dated the jaw to match de Soto's presence.

The Apalachee Indians lived there in about 250 houses with outlying farms, cisterns, and plenty of pottery. They were tall and talented people with a strong civilization.

They had sniped at the invaders all winter with their crossbows. De Soto abandoned the site in 1540, going north to look for gold.

Pensacola Begins and Fails

De Soto did not establish any colonies, but some of his party "discovered" Pensacola Bay. The word of this fine anchorage reached headquarters. In 1559 Tristan de Luna y Arellano set out from Mexico with a fleet of thirteen ships, 500 soldiers, 240 horses, and about 1,000 colonists, including slaves. They had large plans for development.

They stopped at a place, possibly the present day St. Marks, to get water and food for the horses. After this point there was trouble. Many of the horses died, and since they had no reliable charts they confused Mobile Bay with Pensacola Bay and some of the party were separated. Finally, most of the ships were reunited at Pensacola, called Ochuse by the Indians. They picked an idyllic spot for the colony site, but five days later a dreadful hurricane struck.

Alas for de Luna and his numerous companions. Most of the ships, a majority of the people and probably all the supplies were lost. The few survivors, enduring disease, starvation, hostile Indians, and lack of building supplies, did not succeed as a colony. Some of them went on other explorations, many more died, some were rescued, and the colony failed completely. More than a century later, a new Pensacola was established as a major town in Florida history.

The French and Spanish Squabbles

While political and religious quarrels raged in Europe pirates haunted the Florida coast, chiefly lying in wait for the ships headed for Spain with rich cargos of South American and Mexican gold and silver. There was no fixed Spanish colony in Florida.

In France there was not only jealousy of Spanish riches, but there was also internal religious struggle. This was at the period of the Reformation, the rise of Protestantism, in Europe. The new French Huguenots who were Protestants and the established Roman Catholics were bitter enemies. Some of the Huguenots who wanted to escape the turmoil in France tried to establish a colony in Florida, and they caught the Spanish napping.

Right under the careless Spanish noses French colonist Captain Jean Ribault slipped into the mouth of the St. Johns River in 1562 and planted a marker. They didn't set up a colony then but they left their mark of intention. The Timicuan Indians were friendly to these white people who didn't begin at once to fight them. More French came back under a different leader and founded a colony there named Fort Caroline. They called the St. Johns the River of May.

Then the Spanish heard the news!

Ribault arrives in Florida, 1562
Jacques Le Moyne drawing

Pedro Menendez de Aviles

The enraged King of Spain chose Pedro Menendez de Aviles to wipe out the French and establish a permanent Spanish colony with church and fort. Menendez was given the title Captain General of all of Florida.

Menendez had the largest armada of ships and colonists that Florida had ever seen. In 1565 he sailed from Spain with nineteen ships and over a thousand people, including, as usual, women, children, priests and animals. Menendez, sometimes called the founder of Florida and sometimes called the butcher of the Huguenots, was a man who had always lived in the middle of adventure.

To begin with, he was one of twenty siblings, so no wonder he ran away to sea at age fourteen. Now a man of forty-six, he was a keen military strategist, an able administrator, and an adventurous and experienced mariner who had worked on privateer ships and in the treasure fleet of Spain.

The fleet lost ships and met bad weather but better luck came. Not knowing exactly where the French were located, Menendez struck land first around Cape Canaveral and then, going north, found a harbor which he named St. Augustine because it was on that saint's

Pedro Menendez de Aviles lands in Florida, 1567

day in 1565. He rested there a few days, and leaving the non-fighters and some of the crew ashore, he returned to sea to search for the French. When he sighted French ships approaching he hastened back to St. Augustine and hid his ships as best he could, preferring another strategy for his fight.

With a party of 500 men Menendez cleverly set out overland. They hacked their way through the wilderness to make a surprise attack on the French at Fort Caroline which was seriously undermanned since most of their fighting men were at sea looking for the Spanish ships.

The French at the fort were totally unprepared. There are gruesome accounts of the massacre of the French. Menendez was outraged to find some of the French soldiers playing cards with crude pictures of Catholic church leaders printed on them. He said that he killed them "not as Frenchmen but as heretics".

In any case, most of the French were brutally killed. Menendez did not destroy Fort Caroline itself, instead he rebuilt it for Spanish use and renamed it Fort San Mateo.

The Founding of St. Augustine

With the French out of the way for the moment, Menendez set about to finish the other tasks assigned to him. The first was to found St. Augustine, which became the first European town in America to survive. By 1585 St. Augustine had a fort, a council house, a church, dwellings, stores, a school, planned streets, a printing press, community wells and a population of 300 including African slaves. Soon the infamous British pirate Sir Francis Drake slipped in to sack and burn the town, but St. Augustine recovered.

Parts of Old St. Augustine can still be seen today, a monument to the work and wisdom of Menendez. Archaeologists constantly find new evidence of old things, wells, streets, artifacts, pots, pans and even food traces that tell of the sixteenth century Spanish colonial life.

The Artist Jacques Le Moyne

The friendship of the Timucuan Indians paid off for French artist Jacques Le Moyne, a member of the French colony at Fort Caroline. Chief Saturiba was helpful to the artist, who was the first European sent to this country to paint pictures of the native people.

Le Moyne did forty-two drawings and wrote a sympathetic book about the Indians entitled *Narrative of Le Moyne surnamed De Morgues.* Most of the pictures you see of sixteenth century Indians are from this artist. Of course this was before the days of photography.

Le Moyne died in France in 1588 while working on American Indian pictures from field sketches and from memory. His widow sent his work to an engraver, Theodore de Bry, to be copied, but sadly the originals were lost in the transaction. There is only one known remaining original painting, which is now in the New York Public Library.

Le Moyne left America in a big hurry. Why? He was in Fort Caroline when the Spanish arrived to destroy it. Le Moyne was one of the lucky few who jumped over the wall of the fort and escaped to a ship that took him to France before the Spanish could capture him.

The Mission Period

All the Spanish explorers brought missionaries along with them, for the church and state were totally intertwined. Although many soldiers cheerfully cut off the ears, hacked the bodies, enslaved and stole from the Indians, the missionaries wanted to save their souls. The Spanish government paid for the missionaries, and it cost the same to maintain a missionary as a soldier.

As the Indians and the Spanish gradually improved their relationship and garrisons of Spanish soldiers were placed in the seaports and in the wilderness, the Spanish began to build Missions. It seems incredible to us today that North Florida was once peppered with these

Missions, stations with chapels, where soldiers, missionaries and Indians lived.

In 1674, when Bishop Calderon of Cuba was the
religious head of Florida, there were over thirty Missions,
lying from St. Augustine to the Apalachicola River, especially in Leon and Jefferson counties.

The best way to see how the Missions worked is to
visit the partially excavated San Luis de Talamali Mission in Tallahassee, built between 1693 and 1703. There
was an eighty-five by fifty-eight foot blockhouse surrounded by a wooden palisade. Cannons were mounted
for protection and there was a dry moat. There were a
cemetary, a chapel, and sleeping quarters for the staff.
The Indians attached to Missions farmed and were required to contribute food or labor. In return they received protection and help from the soldiers and missionaries

There were often squabbles between the soldiers and
the missionaries. The missionaries were motivated by
faith and religion, but they were political as well. They
felt a stable Mission was a protection against foreign

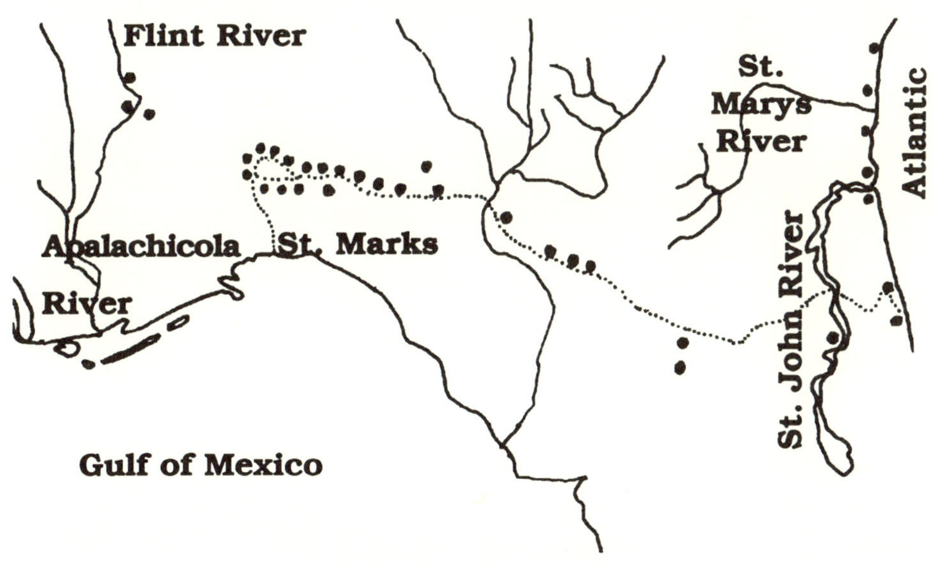

Spanish Missions in 1674

intruders. There were some riots among Indians who felt that they were being used and abused.

The missionaries taught many Indians to speak Spanish, and some Spanish learned the Indian dialects. A certain amount of cultural interchange occurred, and some Indians became staunch allies of the Spanish who taught them farming and a number of European skills.

The first and most famous of the Missions was at St. Augustine, Nombre de Dios, built in 1565 by Menendez. For almost 200 years, Spanish Missions were a vital part of Florida history. Figures vary, but no doubt there were thousands of Indian converts and many instances of true martyrdom by devout missionary priests and lay workers.

One thing the Missions did beside cultural and religious exchanges: they attracted the attention of the British and French who saw the Missions as a proof of Spanish expansion and power.

The British eventually destroyed all the Missions except the one in St. Augustine. Cruel raids by Governor James Moore of North Carolina and by General James Oglethorpe, Governor of Georgia, basically put an end to the Spanish Missions.

If you live in an area where the Missions once flourished, you might discover traces of an old Mission yourself.

The End of the First Spanish Period

From 1700 to 1763 Spanish power in Florida withered away. In 1702 there were about 5000 people in St. Augustine, Spanish colonists, soldiers, and slaves. The only other settlements, Pensacola, and San Marcos de Apalachee, had only a handful of lonesome people. The raids of the English colonies, the struggles with France, pirate attacks, and the decline and loss of the Missions had left a sad situation in the land of the swashbuckling Spanish.

Where the St. Marks and Wakulla rivers met to empty into the Gulf of Mexico there was a good harbor and ample fresh water. There old One-eyed Narvaez had built his flimsy fleet, and other explorers had stopped for water. It was a great hangout for pirates.

Over the years a footpath from St. Augustine had developed to this settlement, then called San Marcos de Apalachee. It had not been a colony nor a planned town. It just happened; it was known and very old, and many Apalachee Indians lived there. In 1679 Spain built a little wooden fort to protect the spot for Spain. When pirates burned the fort a bigger and stronger one was built. Called St. Marks today, this ancient village survived the rise and fall of Spain in Florida.

The major countries in Europe were engaged in the Seven Years War, and the French and Indian Wars were being fought between the French and English colonists in North America in the 1700's. All these battles kept the blood flowing. Although not fought on Florida soil, these wars affected her future.

While the English colonists in the Carolinas and Georgia made raiding and trading forays into Spanish Florida, the angry Spanish looked the other way when runaway slaves from the plantations escaped to freedom in Florida. The Indians were especially sympathetic toward African slaves.

An old Indian settlement, Mose, or Moosa, two miles north of St. Augustine, became a haven for escaped slaves. Mose, the first independent black freedom town in North America, flourished, with many more Indians joining them.

The Spanish were welcoming, and the citizens of Mose were free to mingle with the people in St. Augustine. Finally the Spanish fortified and armed the town, turning it into Fort Mose, for the protection of St. Augustine.

Black soldiers in the uniforms of Spain had guns and other defensive equipment. When Oglethorpe and his forces tried to seize St. Augustine, Fort Mose was the first line of Spanish defense. Finally, when Fort Mose was defeated, the citizens moved into the old fort at St. Augustine. Archaeologists working there today have outlined the town and continually come up with more information about this unique place.

Meantime smugglers and pirates were a constant threat. In one incident in 1739 a British smuggler, Robert Jenkins, was siezed by the Spanish. He claimed that his captors had cut off his ear, which he saved and kept in his pocket until he escaped to England. There was a great uproar in England when he showed this dried-up ear to Parliament in London seven years later. The people demanded "a war for Jenkins' ear". These fights that were tearing up Europe and America were officially ended by the Treaty of Paris in 1763.

In this treaty all of Florida was awarded to England by Spain in exchange for England's Cuba. Spain's 250 year rule in Florida was over!

There was terrible confusion among the people. Most of the displaced Spanish moved to other colonies or mingled with the Indians. A few were allowed to stay in St. Augustine. Spain's flag was hauled down and the British flag went up.

The British were at last in control of Florida, which was immediately divided into two British Crown colonies, the fourteenth and fifteenth "original" colonies in North America, called East Florida and West Florida. Students rarely have been aware of these two additional crown colonies when we speak of the "thirteen original colonies". What happened to number fourteen and fifteen, in the American Revolution, which was not very far down the road?

Chapter Three

British Florida, 1763-1784

British Changes

When the British with their red coats, fifes, and drums moved into Florida, things changed rapidly. If you had lived in Florida then, either at St. Augustine or Pensacola or the neighboring settlements of Mobile or Biloxi, you would think your world had fallen apart.

Actually, it almost did. The government leaders changed, the language changed, the boundaries changed, and religions changed. Most likely you would have moved away to another country entirely, with the total upheaval of leaving your friends, your house, and your favorite spots of land. That is how it is with all displaced people.

In St. Augustine most of the families and soldiers took ships to Cuba and Mexico. There were only 500 people left in the town. In Pensacola they say that there was only one inhabitant left. First, there were boundaries to be established. British Florida was extended west and took in the settlements of Biloxi and Mobile, running all the way to the Mississippi River from the Atlantic Ocean.

South Florida was the mysterious unknown region of alligators, wild Indians, and pirates, and nobody knew much about it, least of all the new owners. The thirty-first parallel was the northern border of Florida which was altered in a few years to give the British more land.

East and West Florida

Florida was then so big that they decided to divide it in half, making it into two colonies, British East Florida and British West Florida, with the Apalachicola River as the dividing point. St. Augustine was the capital of East Florida with her eyes on the Atlantic Ocean, and Pensacola was the capital of West Florida with her attention on the Mississippi River for trade and commerce.

Travel was chiefly by water as there were no broad highways in either Florida, but there were trails worn by Indians and traders on foot and horseback. Eventually, especially where paths and streams met, trading posts grew up, some run by Indians and some by Europeans. These trading centers, where skins and products of the land and forest were traded for manufactured goods, eventually became towns.

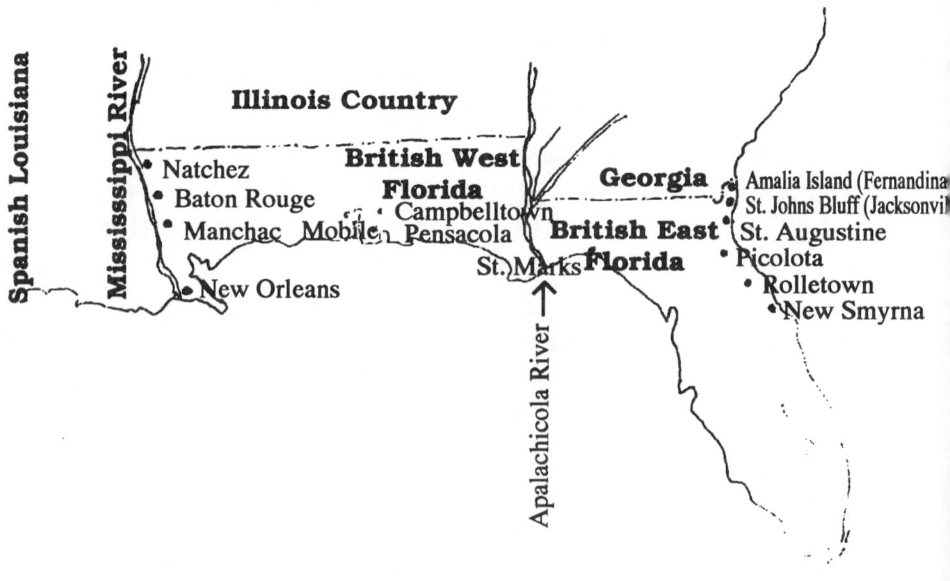

British Florida, 1763-1784

In the two capital towns governments were set up with a governor in each place and other officials sent out from England. There were courts, judges, jails, and some order, but there were not many people. What both Floridas needed desperately was population.

King George III

King George III was the King of England and the King of Florida. This is the same ruler who was despised, burned in effigy, and mocked by the colonial American patriots in the other colonies. But George III showed another side to Florida. He was curious about this new territory he had acquired, and he had a real compassion for the Indians.

He ordered that the British Indian Commissioner hold two conferences with the Indians: one in the Indian village of Picolata for East Florida and one in Mobile for West Florida. The hope of the British government was to establish lasting peace with the Indians and to protect them from dishonest traders. The King also ordered that there would be no more white settlement west of the Mississippi River. This order was never carried out, but with peaceful Indians in the land settlers were more likely to come to Florida.

Indians

In the meantime, in this period of the late eighteenth century, just before the American Revolution, how were the Indians doing?

Most of the aboriginal tribal names that existed when the first Europeans arrived in the 1500's had disappeared, and their descendants, the Upper and Lower Creeks, Chickasaws, Cherokees, and Choctaws lived in tribal groups and were marginally friendly. Only the Miccosukees remained aloof and stuck to their own customs and language.

Some Indians had been forcibly enslaved, especially

in Georgia and the Carolinas where there were big plantations. Many of the Indian slaves ran away to Florida and many of the African slaves came with them. They intermingled and set up their own hidden communities. Out of this situation a new and powerful culture developed, the Seminoles, sometimes called Cimmeroons or Maroons or Siminoles. African or Indian in their ancestry, they were displaced and mostly abused people who formed a powerful new group to be reckoned with.

Strong, bright, survivors, they finally became known as the Seminole tribe. Sometimes when they felt wrongs had been done to them they went on raiding parties, burning lonely farm houses and scalping a few whites. They got a bad reputation in some places and were often feared.

William Bartram

William Bartram

One person who learned to make friends with the Seminoles was William Bartram, a brilliant young botanist and nature lover. We could call him Florida's first environmentalist. His book about Florida, *The Travels of William Bartram* is first- hand information and adventure. Born in Philadelphia in 1739, the son of John Bartram, the foremost botanist in Colonial America, William very early began to observe and sketch the natural world around him. After he finished a good classical Quaker education at nineteen, he went to work as a merchant. He hated it, with all his heart, but his father was determined that his seven sons learn to make enough money to support themselves. He knew from experience that being in love with the environment didn't pay a living. However, his father sent some of his sketches to England where finally William got a sponsor and some money for publications.

George III (remember him?) was also interested in botany so he employed John Bartram, the father, to be a botanist for the King. John Bartram invited his son to be his assistant and the father and son botanist team went to the colony of East Florida which was now only three years old. Through his father's fame and position, William met the most influential people in Florida and learned not only about the natural but also the political scene.

The Bartrams were invited to attend the Indian conference held at Picolata. While the elder Bartram sat in on the negotiations, young William went sketching. When he returned to the group he astonished the Indians and British alike by dragging in a six foot long rattlesnake. He was no longer "the shy boy". The governor was so pleased that he had the snake cleaned and they ate it for dinner.

After the Bartrams returned to Philadelphia, William came back on his own to live with a gun and a pack, a sketch book and Bible in the Florida wilderness.

William travelled mostly alone, by foot, by water, and on horseback. Of course he must have been scared to death of snakes, alligators, and hostile Indians in spite of his reliance on his deep religious faith. Early in his solitary journey near the banks of the St. Mary's River, he saw a big armed Indian on a horse approaching. Bartram tried to hide behind a tree, but the Indian saw him. "I must own that my spirits were very much agitated; I saw at once that, being unarmed, I was in his power," wrote Bartram.

Since he had no time or inclination to prepare his own gun, he walked straight to the frowning Indian, held out his hand and in a quaking voice hailed him as "brother".

The Indian hesitated and then put out his hand, smiled, and the two became friends, exchanging pleasantries as best they could.

Bartram got along well with the Indians, and they gave him the affectionate nickname "Puc-Puggy" meaning one-who-draws-flowers.

Bartram wrote not only of the wild life around him but of chilling fights with alligators, bears, snakes, and storms. Both Indians and the English colonists were hospitable to him but he lived frugally.

His book, still available, was not published until 1791 when he was no longer living in Florida. Other scientists had stolen and claimed credit for some of his works, but over the years people all over the world have read it and discovered the long ago natural marvels of Florida.

Populating the British Floridas

Because the Floridas needed settlers so desperately they gave land grants and made it attractive to settle in the vast territory.

About 100 plantations were established in East Florida. Planters moved in with slaves to try to grow indigo, tobacco, rice, hemp and cotton. The word "plantation" makes us think of mansions and great riches. Actually a plantation is a farm, where like any farm, lots of labor is required to bring crops to harvest.

There was no farm machinery yet, like tractors and reapers and combines, so the large scale planter had to rely on purchased human labor. The institution of slavery of Indians and Africans is reprehensible to us today, but it is a fact of history. Some slaves were imported directly into Florida from Africa. Some were purchased from other colonies. Some were kidnapped Indians. Overseers, sometimes very cruel, had to be employed to control the slaves.

Many people were opposed to slavery or could not

afford slaves. A few small farmers were able to get land and work the soil themselves with the help of sons and daughters, using mules, plows, hoes, and hatchets, if they were lucky enough to have such tools. Over the years a stream of poor landless people drifted into Florida to try for a better life.

Another way of getting new people was to attract wealthy and influential Europeans to set up communities. The British Crown provided the land, and stories of fabulous Florida were published in London. Florida promotion had begun!

The first of the big efforts was the project of Scottish physician Dr. Andrew Turnbull and his partners. In 1768 he brought his Greek wife and 1500 Spanish, Greek, and Italian colonists, about 1200 of whom were from the Spanish island of Minorca where they had suffered a killing famine. They landed below St. Augustine and named the 100,000 acre tract New Smyrna. The colonists were called "indentured servants". There was to be no slavery on this plantation.

Indentured servants were generally poor people who contracted for work in exchange for passage to America. Contracts differed, but many indentured servants were able to buy off their passage in ten or so years and be free to make their fortune in the new country. This was a common practice of the period, but the first such venture in Florida. There were many indentured teenagers, possibly including disguised girls.

The New Smyrna colonists worked hard, were unhappy, and with racial and language differences, soon fell to fighting each other. In the end there was an uprising, the Turnbull mansion was burned, and the remaining few ran away to St. Augustine. One great memorial they left was the famous King's Road, the basis for present State Highway Number Four, that ran from New Smyrna to Georgia. By 1774 the Turnbull community was declared a failure.

Another community in East Florida was established

by Denys Rolle, a philanthrophic Englishman, who was granted land just above Palatka. His colonists were recruited from unfortunates who lived in the gutters of London. The project seemed doomed from the start despite Denys' noble intention to rehabilitate these people with work; he did not believe in slaves. The settlers did not wish to be rescued but preferred their old habits of minor crime to hard work, so Rolle was forced to sacrifice his principles and purchase slaves to keep his plantation going.

The American Revolution and the Floridas

Then the American Revolution came, beginning with the "shot heard 'round the world" at Lexington, Massachusetts, in April 1775.

St. Augustine was very pro-British. When the news of the signing of the Declaration of Independence on July 4, 1776, reached the town Patriots John Hancock and Sam Adams were hanged in effigy in the public square by the Tories.

"Father, what is happening? Why are they hanging stuffed dummies?" cried one little boy.

"They are figures of men who spoke out and were disloyal to England, son. Our family is loyal to the King. Down with the rebels!" replied his father.

Pensacola, the less populated capital of West Florida, was dangerously close to the Spanish in Louisana and New Orleans. The dispossessed Spanish looked longingly across the Mississippi River boundary and said to each other, "We must get our land back".

A word about terms: The Loyalists or Tories were people loyal to England or Britain. The Patriots were American colonials who opposed England in the Revolutionary War.

But the West Florida British persevered in trying to keep peace with the Indians, attract new colonists, and improve the towns. Mobile was part of West Florida now,

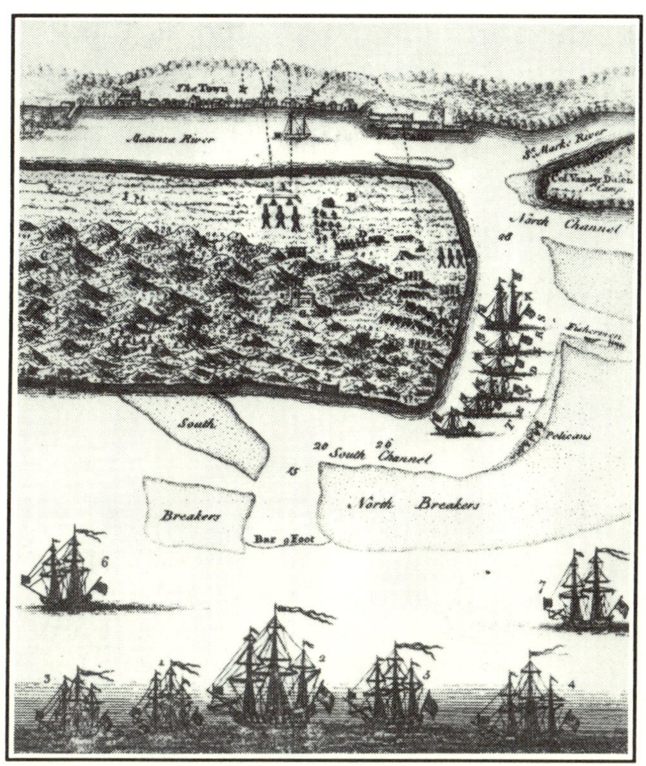

St. Augustine before the American Revolution.

and so were Natchez, Baton Rouge, and Manchac. British businessmen, eager for trade opportunities, arrived from Virginia and other colonies. Grants of land were given, and organized groups of colonists arrived. There was a French community, Campbellton, near Pensacola, where silk and wine culture were attempted, but failed. There were a few Tories from other colonies, but not nearly as many as in East Florida.

Meantime in East Florida, St. Augustine was flooded with an estimated 7,000 Tories, who had been run out or had chosen to leave hostile colonies. Life wasn't too bad. There seems to have been enough food to go around and a need for able workers.

With all the British soldiers in town there was social life with amateur plays and dances. An Anglican Church was established and the old Catholic Church remained. Between the clergy there was some schooling for the children.

There were the usual crimes, some quite serious, and plenty of gossip. Although there were border raids from Georgia there was no notable fighting in East Florida during the Revolutionary War. St. Augustine's sturdy stone fort, Castillo de San Marcos, was a defense as well as a prison. In fact there were some distinguished Patriot prisoners held by the British in the dungeons there, three of whom were signers of the Declaration of Independence.

When Spain and France became allies against Britain, British Florida was doomed. Dashing young Bernado de Galvez, the Spanish governor and military leader from New Orleans, led forces that took Mobile and the other West Florida settlements. Pensacola put up a valiant resistance at Fort George under General John Campbell, but the British Colony of West Florida was defeated in 1781. East Florida did not survive long, for the British forces in North America under Lord Cornwallis surrendered to General George Washington at Yorktown, Virginia, in October, 1781.

Florida's Future

Florida's future was officially settled around a conference table in Paris in 1783 with the new United 'States, Britain, France, and Spain making the decisions. Although the British were to be expelled forever from Florida, it wasn't as simple as it sounds, for once again people were uprooted, property changed hands, and friendships were broken.

The Tories had to find new homes. Many fathers, mothers and children went to the Bahamas, where their descendants live today.

England's twenty years of rule left a mark on Florida's literacy and commerce. Florida's first newspaper *The*

East Florida Gazette, although short lived, began publication in 1783. From West Florida the trading firm of Panton, Leslie, and Company, begun in Pensacola during the Revolutionary War, grew powerful with many branch trading posts. This group had control over Indians, English and Spanish and seemed to survive wars and upheavals in its drive to make money.

And, over the ocean, there was a new governor from Spain on his way to St. Augustine, Vincente Manuel de Zespedes.

Chapter Four

The Second Spanish Period, 1784-1821

Spanish Problems

When the new Governor of East Florida arrived in St. Augustine in 1784, there was a noisy welcome ceremony by Indians, Spanish, and left-over Loyalists or Tories. Governor Zespedes failed to bring the proper presents for the Indians! The Indians were angry, and the Governor lost face.

A sharp British merchant, William Panton, whipped out the right supplies- calico, knives, kettles, ammunition, and trinkets. He saved the day for the Governor and for his firm of Panton, Leslie and Company which got the franchise for all Florida trading posts. He already had the West Florida monopoly. This was real power, and it kept the British influence alive with the Indians.

East Florida had lost most of its population when the Loyalists departed. The Governor wanted new colonists, but he didn't like the people who wanted to come. Americans looked with greedy eyes on Spanish Florida, feeling that this land was theirs by right of location. The British still wanted Florida. Some took oaths of allegiance to Spain, with their fingers crossed, and stayed to be a great nuisance to the new Spanish government. Loyal Spanish colonists did not flock in.

Officially Spain ruled in Florida from 1783 to 1821, when by treaty all of Florida became the territory of the United States. Rule is hardly the right word. By 1800 the huge area of East and West Florida was unmanageable by the governors. There were robbers and raids, pirates and privateers, border battles and brigands. Spanish Florida was out of control. Spain had neither the money nor the power to manage the Indians, the merchants, the threatening Americans, and the lingering power of the British.

Louisiana Purchase

Spain, bankrupt and helpless, ceded Spanish Louisiana to France. This change of power put the American government into an uproar, and President Thomas Jefferson in 1803 countered by making one of the best real estate deals in history. For fifteen million dollars the United States bought Louisiana from France. This was during the Napoleonic Wars in Europe, and France, fearing that England would seize her American lands, accepted the offer quickly.

It was unsettled where the western boundaries lay and whether the deal included West Florida. But in 1810 West Florida declared itself free from Spain and expressed the desire to be annexed to the United States.

Life in West Florida

People then as now had money worries. They wanted, but didn't have, suitable schools for their children, and they struggled for food and secure housing. Indians, Blacks, Spanish, English, and Americans generally feared and mistrusted each other. There were bandits and bad people and snakes and bugs and alligators, a menace to children who wanted to be able to pick blackberries and swim safely. When the men of the area, involved in politics, decided to revolt, the women and children, who had no voice, had to work even harder at farm and household labor in typical frontier style.

Meantime in 1808 the United States had legally stopped importing slaves. Southern planters, who felt a continuous need for the labor of slaves and who were forever losing them over the Florida border, were furious. Slave stealing and runaways increased and neither Spain nor the United States could or would stop it.

The Negro Fort (*renamed Fort Gadsden*)

In the murky political atmosphere of the Floridas in 1816 British, Spanish, Americans, Indians and blacks moved in constant unrest. On Prospect Bluff on the Apalachicola River where East and West Florida were divided, the British built a fort, nominally on Spanish land. They brought mostly slaves of Spanish owners and Indians and then departed leaving the company and a large supply of arms and ammunition behind. It was called the Negro Fort.

Runaway slaves from Georgia, dissident Americans, adventurers, traders, Indians, and anyone else in the

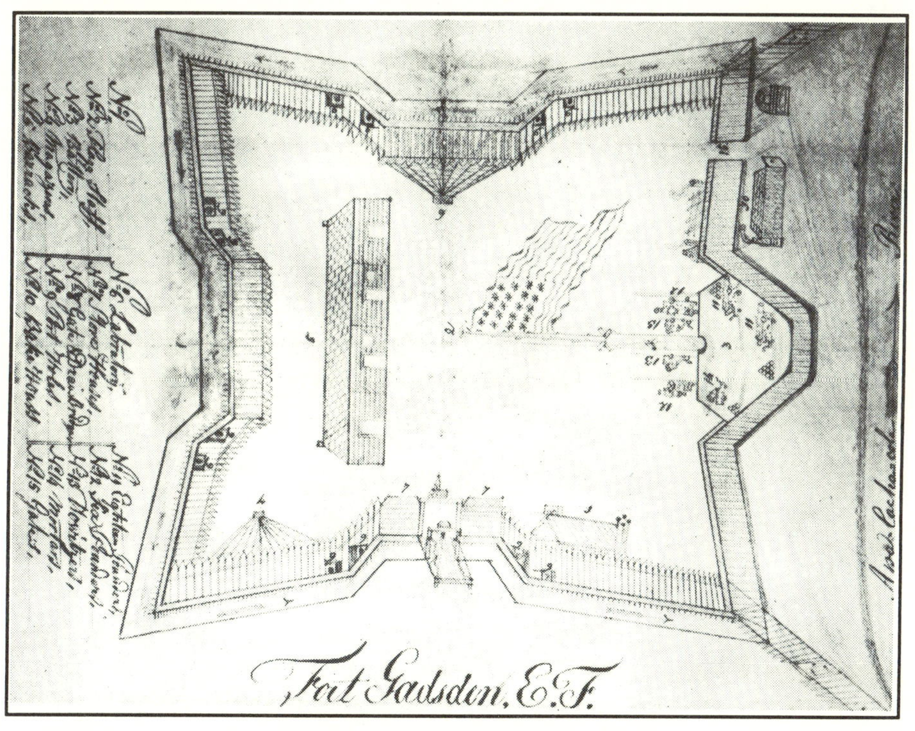

Fort Gadsden, formerly the Negro Fort.

area were free to join the unusual band which scared the Georgia neighbors and interfered with river traffic. The Americans from nearby Fort Scott had difficulties with the Negro Fort, whose leader refused to surrender the fort on demand. A "hot shot", a red hot cannonball, was fired from a river gunboat, causing an explosion heard all the way to Pensacola, The fiery shot hit squarely in the fort's powder magazine, totally blowing up the fort and killing 300 people. Today it is a state historical site renamed Fort Gadsden.

The People Rise Up

Embargoes by the United States caused smuggling and piracy, especially on Amelia Island, a part of East Florida which the British insisted on controlling. This messy situation caused the unruly people to rise up. They called themselves "Patriots". Secretly encouraged by the United States, the Patriots revolted against Spanish rule. The polygot army of 200 easily seized Amelia Island and some land around the St. Mary's River, declaring themselves the "Republic of East Florida". The local American agent accepted the land for the United States, but President James Madison refused this illegal gift.

There were other vivid details of this aborted rebellion, but it is only mentioned here as an example of the unrest and constant political upheaval in Spanish Florida. To top it off, the Creek Indians went on the warpath, fanned up by the British. There was complete anarchy in Florida.

The War of 1812

In 1812 Congress declared war on Great Britain, due to her highhanded conduct on international waters. Southern neighbors were so outraged by the situation in Florida that they hoped for an international war that would force a settlement of the Florida problem. When the War of 1812 ended in 1814, Florida was still in turmoil, but out of this war emerged an American folk figure, Andrew Jackson. An Indian fighter of questionable ethics, he became the President of the United States from 1829 to 1837.

Chapter Five

Territorial Florida

Florida Becomes a Territory

General Andrew Jackson

Major General Andrew Jackson from Tennessee, after taking part in the War of 1812, came to Florida to fight Indians, gathering up much of his army by using anyone who wanted to join the fight. They nicknamed him "Old Hickory".

In 1802 and again in 1805 the United States had tried to buy Florida from Spain, with no success, so the government may have turned a blind eye and a deaf ear to the conduct of the brash general. In 1818 Jackson marched into Spanish Florida, seized the fort at St. Marks, captured Pensacola, killed and executed Indians, burned homes and villages, and took control of this area. He also took two British subjects prisoner and executed them at St. Marks. Congress, Great Britain, and Spain were in a frenzy over these violations of national and international law, but in Washington they reached an agreement. Spain gave over to the United States her rights to the land of Florida, and Congress agreed to pay some debts for Spain. Great Britain let the matter pass.

In 1819 and 1820 the required papers were signed, and the united East and West Florida, now to be governed by Congress with Andrew Jackson as provisional governor, was ready to become a territory of the United States.

In 1821 the Jacksons moved to Pensacola. Mrs. Jackson, a lady of sturdy manners whose tastes ran to smoking her own pipe, watched with her husband as the Stars and Stripes replaced the Spanish flag on July 17, 1821. A similar ceremony occurred in St. Augustine, and a quiet transfer took place in the old fort at St. Marks.

The Seminole Wars, Wars of Indian Removal

There were three periods of fighting in Florida between Americans and Indians, usually called the Seminole Wars, or more accurately, "The Wars of Indian Removal". These conflicts were caused principally by two pressures. The first was to recover slaves who had escaped from planters in the southern states and made their way to Florida where they were either treated as free people or as slaves of the Indians. The second was to get more Indian lands to use as plantations. As mentioned earlier, the United States had prohibited the direct importation of more African slaves in 1808, and planters who were farming large areas needed slave and household labor to support their lifestyle.

Before the plantation owners are completely condemned, consider the non-slave northeast states, which were then going into the Industrial Revolution. The factory owners also required cheap laborers, so they often resorted to child labor, new immigrants, sweatshops,

A battle in the Seminole Wars

cruel foremen and the economic slavery of low wages, poor working and living conditions. Neither system is legal today.

The first Seminole War was the brief and stormy excursion of Andrew Jackson into Spanish Florida. General Jackson had earlier defeated the Creeks at the bloody Battle of Horseshoe Bend in Alabama and dictated a treaty in which they gave up about two-thirds of their tribal lands. Naturally the surviving Indians who moved into Florida hated Andrew Jackson. Florida's family album, like that of most families, contains individuals who are admirable as well as those who are somewhat objectionable. Andrew Jackson may well fall into the latter category, having been described by Florida historian Kathryn Abbey as having "...complete confidence in emotion and prejudice as a substitute for information and law..."

The Indians were forced to move once again when the site for the Florida capital was chosen, although the Indian Removal Act of 1830 permitted them to exchange their lands for new lands in Oklahoma. Some of the chiefs signed treaties in 1832, but the Seminole Nation rejected the treaties, and the Second Seminole War, a long and bloody conflict, started in 1835. Both sides fought with flint lock muzzle-loading rifles plus some cannon on the side of the Americans. Bows and arrows were used by the Indians when silence was essential or powder scarce. Battles were often ambushes, with hidden warriors opening fire on unsuspecting troops, many of whom were casualties of the first surprise volley.

Indian Commissioner Wiley Thompson, and a Lieutenant Smith, while strolling some 300 yards from Fort King on December 28, 1835, were killed. On the same day, Major Francis Dade and two companies of regular U.S. troops were attacked and only two badly wounded privates survived. Three days later General Duncan Clinch and a substantial American force were attacked by some 250 warriors under Osceola and Alligator at the Withlacoochee River. The Indians were driven off but not defeated.

The Seminoles were often led by Billy Powell, a Red Stick Creek, also known as Osceola. He had been a sub-chief under Chief Micanopy. A determined and charis-

Osceola and his chiefs

matic leader, he quickly became the most important and successful Seminole chief. Forces under Osceola killed several Indian leaders who were negotiating to move west, as well as substantial numbers of United States regular and militia forces.

One of the reasons that large numbers of Indians refused to honor treaties of removal signed by some of their leaders was the matter of African slaves either owned or assimilated by the Indians. These slaves owned by the Indians were usually quite independent and relatively well treated and were certainly opposed to being returned to plantation slavery. Intermarriage between Indians and escaped African slaves was not unusual. Slave hunters and planters of course wanted all the slaves to be returned to the slave markets and plantations.

In 1837 Osceola asked for a meeting near St. Augustine. While under the white flag of truce, he was captured by American forces and put in prison, first at St. Augustine, then at Charleston, S.C. where he died a short time later. Another leader, a young chief named Coacoochee or Wildcat, was also captured but managed to escape the St. Augustine prison to lead the Seminoles through the rest of the war. By 1842, Wildcat had been captured and sent to Oklahoma, and many other Indian leaders had been killed, so the War Department announced that the Second Seminole War had ended. This war was expensive, not only because of the funds spent and the lives lost, but also because new settlers were afraid to move into this region making Central Florida lands virtually worthless.

When Florida became the twenty-seventh state in the United States in 1845 people hoped to settle down peacefully to exploit the rich lands and favorable climate of the state. However, in 1855, U.S. Army surveyors deliberately destroyed the garden of Chief Billy Bowlegs in the Big Cypress Swamp just to see him "cut up". When he demanded money and apologies for this destruction, this peaceful chief was pushed around and humiliated by the army men, until he departed to start the Third Seminole War in southern Florida. Indian removal was more important than killing in this war, for rewards were offered for captured Indians. In 1858, after forty-one Seminoles were captured, Billy Bowlegs consented to go west taking 165 Seminoles with him to Oklahoma. This ended the Third Seminole War. The Seminoles who remained in Florida reservation areas eventually ended up as tourist attractions, wrestling alligators and selling souvenirs and postcards.

The Story of Milly Francis

Milly or Malee Francis was the beautiful daughter of Chief Francis the Prophet, also called Hillis Hadjo. She lived in her father's village near St. Marks when the First Seminole War began. Her father's warriors captured a young Georgia soldier, Duncan McKrimmon, and were preparing to execute him when Milly came on the scene and pled that his life be spared. Her father agreed that

Milly Francis pleads for the life of Duncan McCrimmon

this could be done if a ranson was paid for his life, and Milly persuaded the Spanish commandant of the St. Marks fort to negotiate with her father's warriors. Finally, for a ransom of seven and one half gallons of rum, paid by the Spanish, McKrimmon was released.

Milly later served as an interpreter for British Captain Robert Ambrister while he was at St. Marks, where he was tried and executed by Andrew Jackson. Her father, Chief Francis was also hanged by Jackson at St. Marks without trial. Milly went to Oklahoma a few years later and was eventually recognized there by an Army officer who had served in Florida and, at his request, awarded a pension and medal by Congress.

The Trial of Ambrister at St. Marks

More About Slavery

While slaves worked on the plantations and the United States Army and the Florida volunteers wiped out or drove out the Indians, many citizens in Florida and the rest of the world objected to the violation of the rights of the Indians and Africans. Benevolent societies, abolitionists, and missionaries tried to change the system of slavery and Indian removal.

There were many slave owners who were troubled with the system too, but it was illegal to set a slave free without complex court permission, and it was prohibited to teach slaves to read and write. Freed slaves had a hazardous life, often being picked up as runaways. Some slave owners secretly taught their slaves to read even though it may have been dangerous to do so. Slave owners lived in constant dread of slave uprisings.

If a slave ran away, as they often did, or was kidnapped, this was a serious financial loss to the owner, especially if a bank had lent money on a slave. Slaves

U.S. Marines in the Seminole Wars

could be mortgaged, the same as any property. Slave owners paid rich rewards for the return of slaves, and being a "slave hunter" was a profitable business.

Owners were responsible for the health and welfare, clothing, food, housing, and legal justice for their slaves. There were laws protecting the slaves, which were mostly obeyed. A man could whip his slaves but not kill them. It was a terrible life to be either a slave or a slave owner.

The Declaration of Independence of the United States says: "We hold these truths to be self-evident, that all men are created equal, that they are endowed by their Creator with certain unalienable Rights, that among these are Life, Liberty, and the pursuit of Happiness."

Yet neither the Declaration of Independence nor the original Constitution forbids slavery. Many of the framers of both were slave owners themselves. Most likely the oversight was that in the late 1700's only white men were considered human. These were not considered evil men, but by training and tradition they assumed that rights belonged to them. Blacks, women, and Indians did not count for the "unalienable rights". Within this system there were still kindnesses, personal friendships, and compassion among all classes and colors, but this was not required by law.

The Indians, who had once lived in chiefdoms and villages around their sacred mounds, were now people on the run, a people in hiding, a people with their hunting customs and ancestors destroyed with the seizure of their lands. Indian traditional culture was no longer possible. Gone were the well crafted wood and wattle houses in stable villages, unique pottery and carvings, and safe hours of leisure for historic story telling around a campfire. At the end of the Seminole Wars in the 1850's, the Americans had "won" a hollow victory since the Indians were dead or removed to Oklahoma, except for a few who lived in the Everglades or were half hidden in a few scattered villages or in some unexplored regions of South Florida.

One little footnote of Florida history, not well known, is that ex-slave Africans themselves owned some plantations and used Indian and maybe some African slave labor. These plantations were mostly found around Sarasota Bay. Both Seminoles and runaway or freed slaves had sought refuge in South Florida. Some blacks had fought with the British and been defeated in the War of 1812 (especially at New Orleans where Andrew Jackson defeated the British in the famous battle fought after peace was declared in Washington, without Jackson's knowledge). In the terrible confusion following this battle a group of blacks was able to sail to Tampa Bay, where there had long been a black haven, and set up a farming community. The Africans and Indians had always maintained a unique slave and owner relationship, as has been referred to earlier, where the two groups shared products and friendship, not as traditional slave and master.

The Sarasota area continued as a central area for runaway slaves. The plantations here were in operation for several years. Inevitably as the American settlers gained access to this area and the presence of the hidden enclave of runaway or freed slaves became known, the blacks were driven out. However, the blacks, Cuban fishermen, and Indians all intermarried and protected each other until they became a whole new set of settlers who melted into the landscape they called home.

Governing Territorial Florida, 1821-1845

At first the Florida people had few political rights. The President of the United States appointed the Governor and other officials. Self government was a gradual process to statehood.

"We need more rights, freedom to make decisions like the other Americans have," grumbled some of the people. But Florida was a territory, not a state, and so it would be until statehood came in 1845.

U.S. Encampment at Picolata in the Seminole Wars

There were an estimated 5,000 white citizens in Florida then. Neither Indians nor slaves could vote nor were they counted in the casual census as they were not considered citizens. Probably the number of human beings in Florida was twice that number.

In 1821 there were only two towns of any consequence, Pensacola and St. Augustine, which were 400 miles apart. The President appointed the Territorial Council, which met in 1822 in Pensacola. The President also appointed William P. DuVal from Virginia and Kentucky to be the first Territorial Governor.

When the second Council session met in 1823 in St. Augustine, the unanimous first order of business was to establish a central capital city. There had to be a more convenient place not requiring a long sea journey or pioneering through jungles to get to the meetings.

John Lee Williams, a lawyer and business man from Pensacola, and Dr. William Hayne Simmons from St. Augustine were chosen for the task of finding a suitable spot somewhere between the Ochlocknee and Suwannee Rivers. The men planned to meet at St. Marks on the Spanish road that had been "improved". That meant that the engineer in charge was to leave no tree stumps higher than two feet in the roadway. Think of that, people who now complain of bumps and potholes!

Dr. Simmons took the overland route on horseback, leaving St. Augustine on September 26, 1823. There were the usual hazards of bugs, angry Indians, and highway robbers for his party, but he arrived in St. Marks on October 10.

Williams and party left Pensacola on September 24 in an open boat. They were shipwrecked, marooned, persecuted by insects and storms, but reached St. Marks late in October.

After a brief rest the men moved twenty miles north to the rich hilly country where Jackson had destroyed a prosperous Indian town.They chose a site which they estimated to be about half way between St. Augustine and Pensacola and began to stake out the town of Tallahassee, the new capital of Florida. They persuaded the few remaining Indians to move out. By 1824 the third Territorial Council met in the new location.

Tallahassee soon became a social, agricultural and political center as the people moved in. It was surrounded by rich lands, and the climate made a natural spot for new cotton plantations. Towns were springing up and growing nearby, Apalachicola, Monticello, Port Leon, Marianna, St. Joseph and Magnolia, to name a few. In Key West, far to the south, the old settlement was growing, more Cuban than American. Real estate promotion, Florida's specialty, began to blossom.

As towns grew up, so did small newspapers. Almost every town had one or more newspapers which were great local promoters. When one town had yellow fever, the local paper hesitated to publish that news, but it was always ready to let the citizens know that the next town was in bad shape. Rivalry for new settlers was carried out in the papers. Some towns simply died out from yellow fever and hurricanes. Two that totally disappeared were Magnolia and Port Leon, once flourishing cotton towns near St. Marks, now only marked by old graves and a few copies of their newspapers.

The newspapers carried news about slavery and abolitionists, advertisements of the latest fashions, and rewards for runaway slaves. Horror stories about Indian reprisals and the Indian wars, shipping and financial news, and many pious moralistic stories were popular. There was little national or world news overall, and editorials were seldom of lasting importance. Notices of bank failures and obituaries were always keenly read.

The newspapers indicate that there was a reading public even in this rough hewn society. In the Territory of Florida before 1845, for varying periods of time, there were forty-four newspapers published in a dozen towns.

Newcomers From France

After the end of the Revolutionary War the grateful United States gave a grant of land to the Marquis de Lafayette, the French General who so nobly helped the American cause. Lafayette was a great hero, whose charm spread when he made a triumphal tour of the south. In 1824 Lafayette was given a grant of land in the center of Leon County, as a result of the influence of Richard Keith Call, a prominent territorial citizen. Lafayette was an abolitionist so he refused to use slaves, instead importing sixty French peasants to cultivate his land. The plan did not succeed but the effects on land sales, titles and surveys have been a headache to the present day. Lafayette himself never came to Florida.

A Frenchman who caused a flutter in Tallahassee was Prince Achille Murat, a nephew of Napoleon who, forced to leave his own country, chose to settle in Florida in the 1820's. He married a beautiful local widow Catherine Willis Gray. Murat said he did not believe in slavery, but he succumbed to the system and owned slaves. His house is still standing, moved to a new location at the Tallahassee Junior Museum.

From royalty to renegades, new settlers continued to arrive in the Territory. Streams of new plantation owners with slaves and families bought up fertile lands in Leon, Jefferson, Gadsden, Madison and other counties in north Florida.

In 1834 the Tallahassee Railroad Company went into operation. The wooden cars were pulled by mules over iron strips from Tallahassee to St. Marks, a distance of twenty miles. There was one passenger car with eight wooden bench seats. The rest of the train was for hauling cotton from the plantations in the hills to the port at St. Marks where it was shipped to northern factories. Fifty

Tallahassee-St. Marks Railroad Co. terminal in Tallahassee

thousand bales a year was the average shipment on this little train. It was the only railroad in operation when Florida became a state, although there were other trials and errors that did not last. It was said that this was the most wretchedly uncomfortable train the entire world has ever known as it crawled, lurched, bumped and banged its way through the swamps and brush. The old railroad right-of-way, made smooth, is now a bicycle and hiking path.

The Story of Alonzo DeMilt

One group of settlers who sailed from New York into Port Leon in 1839, were Alonzo DeMilt, age eight, and his little sisters Elizabeth and Frances with their parents. Many years later in 1883 Alonzo wrote a book *The Life, Travel, and Adventures of an American Wanderer*, which documents this family saga in territorial Florida. It is not clear why the DeMilt family came to Port Leon, a thriving cotton port. They were well-to-do New Yorkers, socially prominent; perhaps they came for health reasons or to mourn the recent death of another child. Or maybe they came to make money in real estate. Some people did.

Alonzo de Milt

The DeMilts built a house in the center of Port Leon, probably of logs, across the street from a sailors' tavern where people from the nearby villages of Magnolia and St. Marks came to drink and brawl and sing bawdy songs far into the night. There was no police control, no church, no bank, and no jail in this town.

Two years after the family arrived there was a killing yellow fever epidemic. Within a few days Alonzo's father and mother and sister Frances lay dead, and ten year old Alonzo and his little sister Elizabeth were left orphaned strangers in a strange land.

Mr. Densmore, who owned the tavern, and other neighbors saw to burying the dead parents and child. A kind widow, Mrs. Spencer, took the toddler Elizabeth, and Densmore himself took over the care of the orphaned boy. Densmore, however, had evil designs. He turned little Alonzo into a barkeeper's slave.

Alonzo decided to have none of that. After a few months of ill treatment and sorrow over his parents, he begged help from David Kennedy, the keeper of the St. Marks lighthouse. Because Densmore was holding Alonzo prisoner he had to hide himself in Kennedy's boat to escape.

The Kennedy family treated him kindly, but Alonzo decided to run away to join his relatives in New York. To do this he determined to get help from his father's friend, a military officer at Fort Stansbury, an Indian fighting fort in the area. So off he ran. He liked his life on the military post, and even found his sister there, being cared for by another family.

The officer took the boy in and let him live in the barracks with him. When the troops moved, Alonzo moved with them, watching the fighting and negotiations with the Indians. In 1843, when Alonzo was with the troops in Cedar Key, they lashed him to a tree and saved his life while a violent hurricane tore up the coast. It was such a terrible storm that the town of Port Leon was blown away; even graves were washed out to sea.

When Alonzo's benefactor took a wife, Alonzo ran away again. He was eventually reunited with his family in New York. His adventures don't end there, according to his published life story. He took part in the California gold rush, travelled all over the world, and eventually became important in the government of Australia. With luck you might find an old copy of this self-told adventure of a Florida pioneer in a dusty attic or library.

A Little Historic Fiction on the Eve of Statehood

The place, the time, and the people:
A plantation in Jefferson County,
Territory of Florida, November, 1838.

Uncle Curtis, the oldest slave on the place, sat hunched over a polished pine board in his lap, his old hand deftly moving a charcoal pencil. Uncle Curtis had come down from South Carolina with the family when they had moved by wagons to the Florida frontier, with animals, furniture, tools, and people both black and white.

Plantation scene

69

"What are you drawing, Uncle Curtis?", asked Tom, climbing down from the pecan tree where he had been shaking nuts for the dozen or so children to put into their baskets.

"I'm making a picture of you children," said Uncle Curtis. "I guess I'm starting Florida's family album. All of you, black, white, Indian, Spanish, French, you're Florida's past and future, one family."

"I don't believe that for one minute," said Mary Ellen, Tom's saucy younger sister. "How can we be one family if we're not even the same color?"

"Makes no nevermind, child," said Uncle Curtis. "Come here closer, little Beaver. I want to draw you."

Beaver, a Miccosukee Indian boy shyly moved up to the old man's knee. "Your people left you behind by mistake, didn't they?", said Uncle Curtis.

"Yes sir," said Beaver. "My sister Bird and I were hiding from the troops when they drove the last of our people out of here. We'll go find them some day. We heard they live in a big swamp down south now. Big Willie took us in and we live with the slaves now. But we're not slaves."

Tom and Mary Ellen's mother, the mistress of the plantation, walked over from the big house. It was a simple dwelling, made of cypress logs, with open porches front and back and a "dog trot" open hall through the center. The kitchen was a separate little cabin in the back yard.

"Mary Ellen, take off your good shoes! You know you can't be pecan picking in your Sunday shoes. Get barefooted like the rest of the children," she scolded.

"But it's cold, it's November, Ma'am," argued Mary Ellen.

Her mother looked at her sternly, and Mary Ellen slowly removed her red leather shoes, a gift from her Charleston grandmother.

"Uncle Curtis, your picture tells a wonderful story," exclaimed Ma'am. "You have a great talent. What an assortment of young Florida pioneers!" She glanced about her at the group. There were her own two children; the Miccosukee pair; two little blonde tow heads from Appalachia, children of the plantation overseer; a cousin from Pensacola, descendant of British Tories, and his two Spanish stepbrothers from an old Pensacola family; and six black children born into slavery. There was one beautiful tan mulatto girl, whose mother was the cook; and one French orphan girl, a teenaged remote cousin from Georgia who had nowhere else to live.

With deft marks Uncle Curtis captured on his slab of wood the spirit of the group. The pecans the children gathered that day were to be shipped north in burlap bags with the cotton bales from the Port of St. Marks.

"Maybe they'll go on the *Newcastle* with Father and the other delegates to the convention at St. Joseph and then on to the big ports in New England", said Tom. "Father's going to let me ride in the wagon to St. Marks and help bring the mules back".

Plantation children

"Father's going to miss the Christmas parade in town", said Mary Ellen sadly.

"I know," said Ma'am, "but he has serious government business to do for our Florida Territory. Our leading men are going to write a constitution so we will be ready to become the State of Florida and not just a territory anymore."

"Tell me about your Christmas parade," said Johnny, the cousin from Pensacola. His father was also going to the convention, while Johnny and his stepbrothers visited on the plantation.

"It's good!" cried Tom. "The slaves get a holiday, and all of us dress up in costumes and do all kinds of tricks. And there are presents for everyone, and sugar cane, and songs and banjos play. And we make candy with pecans in it. Oh, Christmas is wonderful here in Florida."

"Time to quit, the nuts are ready for the baggers," called Uncle Curtis. He rose stiffly, carefully protecting his charcoal drawing as he moved to his cabin.

The children scampered away to get ready for their suppers. If they were lucky they might have grits and red-eye ham gravy, some corn bread or biscuits, turnip greens or collards, and maybe some venison or a bite of sausage. With real luck there might be molasses pecan pie. "After supper we can go see the ruins of an old Spanish mission," said Tom to his Pensacola cousin. "It's over that hill in the woods."

"Do you think any Indians will catch us and scalp us in the dark?" asked the visitor.

"I hope not," said Tom nonchalantly. "We'll take my dog and a lighted pine knot."

"There are Spanish ghosts over there," warned Mary Ellen.

"Have you ever seen any friction matches, the kind you just strike a light with?" asked Johnny as they walked through the darkening woods.

"No," said Tom. "We just take our lights from the kitchen fire. But I read about those. Maybe we'll get some when we're grown up. I hope we have peace and safety when we grow up."

A screech owl let out his deathly cry. It must have been the Spanish ghost telling them that peace and safety were not coming soon.

The First Constitutional Convention, 1839-1840

The Constitutional Convention was held to draft a basic document which would organize the territory to function as a state. Some grumbled that it was held in the remote new village of St. Joseph.

Many of the elected delegates objected to the travel difficulties they had to endure to reach the place located on the Gulf of Mexico west of Appalachicola.

Some went by horseback or carriage, some by ships and stage coach. All were travel weary when they finally

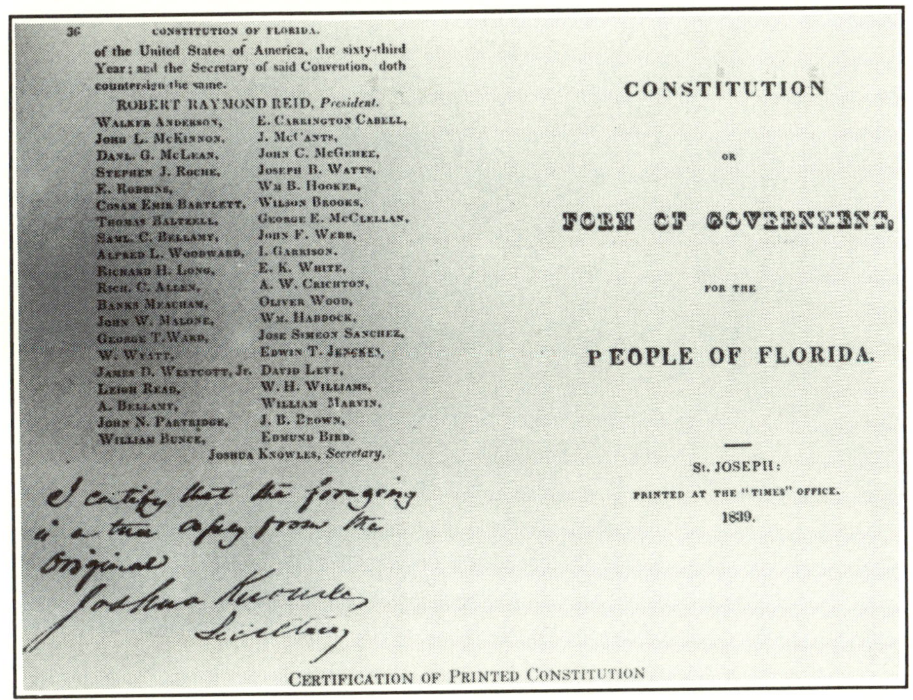

Florida's first constitution, 1839

arrived and found that the St. Joseph promoters had built a special convention hall, decorated with leaders' pictures, as well as some boarding houses and hotels. Periodic efforts were made to adjourn the convention at St. Joseph and reconvene at Tallahassee but all failed.

Territorial Florida was, by now, politically divided into East Florida, the area east of the Suwannee River; Middle Florida, the area between the Suwannee and Apalachicola Rivers; and West Florida, lands west of the Apalachicola.

The elected delegates, representing each of the Florida counties in rough proportion to their estimated population, included lawyers, planters, ministers, newspaper editors, medical doctors, an innkeeper, a sea captain and fisherman, and a merchant. Of the total number of fifty-six elected as delegates, forty-six showed up at the scheduled opening of the convention on December 3, 1838. The following day the convention considered the first of the numerous issues that faced them, the selection of proxies to vote for the absent delegates. The final choice of proxies probably influenced the election of the Convention President, which ended up with Robert R. Reid defeating William P. DuVal by one vote.

Committees were appointed from among the delegates and each was assigned the task of drafting a given portion of the future Constitution. Some committees came up with appropriate portions of the Alabama Constitution, while others, dealing with controversial provisions, fought and debated their assigned areas.

Most of the delegates were very pro-slavery. The convention was divided on the question of whether Florida really wanted to be a state or to remain a territory for a longer time. The most controversial area was the regulation of the banking industry. Both the nation and the Territory of Florida had recently undergone a period of depression and bank failures. The Territory of Florida, through the Legislative Council, had issued substantial bond issues to raise money for the three major territorial banks.

After long fiery debates, sarcasm, and name-calling, a compromise was finally agreed upon which enabled the future state to regulate new banks but not to interfere with existing contracts, which included these bank bond issues. It is ironic that these three banks had all failed and were out of business before Florida's statehood.

The Convention finally finished a draft of a state Constitution and adopted it on January 10, 1839, with all except one delegate voting for it. The one dissenter was opposed to the bank clause. The Convention adjourned the next day, and the weary delegates departed.

The proposed Constitution'was submitted to Florida voters on the first Monday in May, 1839, and was narrowly approved by the people. Many districts which had advocated the drafting of a constitution were not satisfied with the final product. After the usual disagreement on the validity of some of the votes, the Constitution, finally proclaimed as having been ratified on October 21, 1839, was forwarded to the U. S. Congress.

Chapter Six

Florida Becomes a State

Statehood

Not everybody wanted the Territory of Florida to become a state. First, the United States government deliberated, because Florida was a slave area. The practice then was that if a slave state was admitted, a non-slave state had to come in at the same time.

Then the people in Florida themselves had divided opinions. The people in East Florida wanted Florida to come in as two states, East and West. Some people wanted Florida to become part of Alabama or Georgia. Some thought taxes would rise. Some thought they'd get bossed around by the Federal government.

There were rallies, caucuses, committees, and quarrels. There were two main political parties, the Whigs and the Democrats. They didn't agree on many issues, and the political climate was hot.

Finally it was ironed out. Iowa, a non-slave territory wanted to get into the Union too. Florida pushed its internal disagreements under the rug, with much work on the part of David Levy Yulee, the Florida delegate to Congress. He pointed out that there would be Federal lands available, schools would be under local control, people could vote for their own officials, and have a voice in national affairs. In January 1845 the Territory made a formal request for statehood; so did Iowa. Events worked fast in the United States Senate and House, and on March 3, 1845, President John Tyler signed the act of admission for Florida. The news reached Florida by mail on March 8. The telegraph had not yet come to Florida although it had been invented in 1835.

The population of Florida at this time was in question for there had never been a reliable census. David Yulee assured (with crossed fingers, it was rumored) that the population of the Territory was 90,000. A later census indicated that this was a great exaggeration.

Now Florida had to get its political parties together, find candidates, and have primary elections and a general election with votes by the people just as elections are held today. There was some mud slinging and some name calling but the Democrats won, and William D. Moseley became Florida's first elected governor.

When the new governor was inaugurated in Tallahassee on June 25, 1845, there was a great celebration and a new Capitol. There were crowds of visitors, decorations, speeches, and people marching and tooting horns and beating drums. The ladies were beautiful and the gentlemen were charming. Probably a few were tipsy. Cannons were fired, and after a splendid parade of soldiers, clergy, politicians, boy students and twenty-eight school girls, representing the twenty-six old states and the two new ones, people took their places in front of the Capitol, and the new governor was sworn in. Florida was now the twenty-seventh state of the Union. There were still a few offices to fill, but the situation was stable with the government in place and functioning. The only sad news on that day was that President Andrew Jackson, "Old Hickory", had died at his home in Tennessee.

Dr. Gorrie's Ice Machine

Whenever you take a deep breath of cold air in Florida in midsummer by the flick of a switch, think of Dr. John Gorrie, born about 1802, who invented artificial ice and air conditioning. Dr. Gorrie came to Apalachicola in 1833 soon to become a leading citizen, mayor, postmaster, physician, pharmacist, church founder, civic leader, and inventor. His medical practice flourished, but his heart was in research for the victims of malaria and yellow fever.

Dr. Gorrie married and built a large house with a few extra rooms for a laboratory and sick patients. He found that keeping fever patients cool and dry would help or even cure them. He urged the town to clean up swamps and wet areas. His studies showed him that these diseases did not occur in dry cold northern climates.

"We need ice and room coolers in Florida," he told himself and then set about to try to manufacture them.

In those days only natural ice was known. In cold New England enterprising farmers cut ice blocks from their ponds in winter for shipment in insulated ships to southern ports. Ice was so expensive that few Floridians ever saw any. Only once in a blue moon did an ice ship come to Apalachicola.

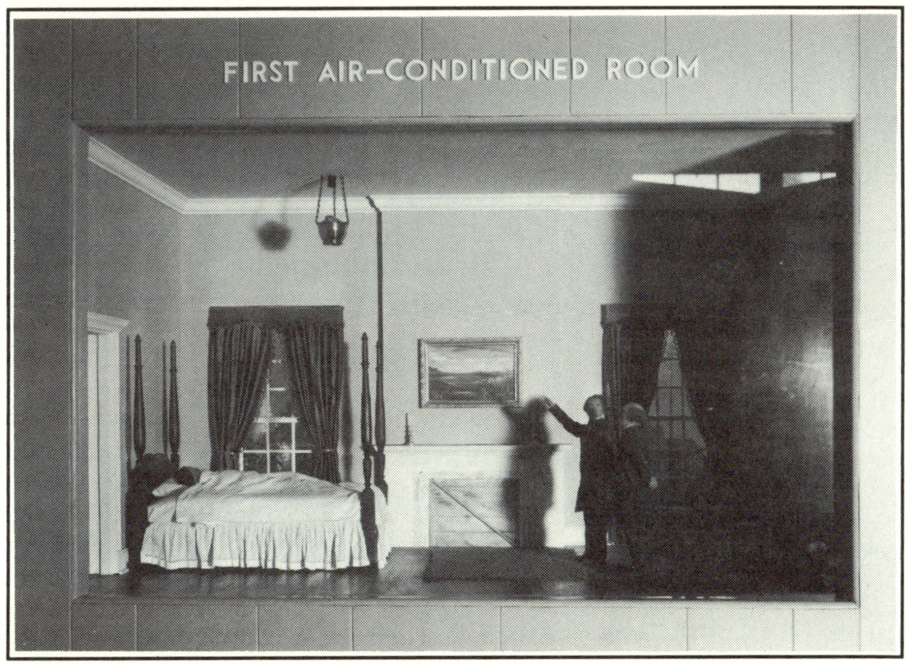

A representation of Florida's first air-conditioned room,
Gorrie Museum, Apalachicola

Gorrie gave up his time and almost all of his medical practice to work on the invention of ice machines. He used all his funds and all his wife's money, and finally built a machine that would manufacture ice and cool a room by removing heat from water with an air compression method. It was basically a simple and natural process, but he needed financial backers. He got patents in America and England in 1851, but they expired twenty years later for lack of production.

Ice is such a blessing in hot climates that today we are amazed that the ice machine didn't have instant success. Gorrie was blocked by a greedy group of ice boat skippers who saw bankruptcy for their small industry if artificial ice succeeded.

"Make ice in Florida in July? Ha ha ha", was the response of potential backers who read silly stories of Gorrie's invention in northern newspapers.

Gorrie died in 1855 without seeing the eventual success of his invention. When ice production caught on, southern towns built ice plants, and in the early twentieth century wagons with blocks of ice for home delivery were a common sight. Children loved to sneak under the ice houses or wagons for chips of ice.

Today in Florida almost every home has an ice making refrigerator and air conditioning. Dr. Gorrie is honored in the Statuary Hall in the nation's Capitol for the benefits he gave to the world. In Apalachicola there is a museum in his memory where the first ice machine is on display.

From Statehood to Secession

Only fifteen years after Florida became a member of the United States, she wanted out. Most Floridians wanted slaves and the right of the state to make that decision more than she wanted to be a part of the Union. There were still many loyal "Unionists".

"Secession", withdrawing, was the word on all lips,

pro or con. It seemed every household and village had different ideas. By no means was there one unified Florida opinion, even after the Civil War erupted. The opinions of slaves and women were not considered. Hampered by illiteracy, both slaves and poor whites, had little access to information. The rest of the world considered Florida "backward". Houses were lit with candles or fireplaces until kerosene lamps came to a few families about 1860.

Abolitionists were people who tried to force the end of slavery in the United States in a missionary effort. Naturally the local people resented this outside interference with their way of life. A notable abolitionist, Harriet Beecher Stowe, a New Englander who wrote the famous novel about slavery, *Uncle Tom's Cabin*, angered slave holders. However, Mrs. Stowe herself was a kind and intelligent woman who loved Florida and wanted to help the situation. After the Civil War she bought a house on the St. Johns River and became a Florida promoter.

Another abolitionist was the popular Northern poet John Greenleaf Whittier, who wrote long narrative po-

The branding of Jonathan Walker

ems with stern moral lessons. His poem "The Branded Hand" swept the country to tell the story of an obscure white Massachusetts farm boy, Jonathan Walker, who came to Pensacola to work as a seaman and ship builder. He saw no difference between black and white skin, and when he bought a little house in Pensacola he rented rooms to freed slaves, entertained them and employed them for his ship building business.

This unusual social conduct annoyed people in Pensacola. Finally he decided to move his family back north. Seven of his black friends engaged him to help them escape in his boat to Nassau and freedom, an illegal action. This Walker agreed to do, but the little boat was caught near Key West, and he was brought back to prison and a horrible punishment.

With a hot iron, the letters "S S" were branded on his hand, meaning that he was a slave stealer. Famous people all over the world took up his cause, paid his fines and defense costs. His story had its effect on Florida and

Cowboys wrestling a bull, a drawing by Frederick Remington

the whole United States and became the conscience of the anti-slavery movement.

During this period Florida grew, especially now that southern Florida had become free of Indian raids. The Peace River area began to prosper, built on a beef growing economy rather than cotton. Beef was to be of great importance for feeding both Confederate and Union armies in a few years.

A few more roads were constructed and a crude railroad "system" developed, connecting Fernandina, Cedar Key, Jacksonville, and Tallahassee with steam engine pulled trains. The old mule drawn cotton train from St. Marks to Tallahassee, struggled along, the butt of continuing jokes and local legends. One traveller, arriving in St. Marks by ship, tried to ride the train to Tallahassee to complete his journey. There were so many disasters on the trip that in disgust the stranger got off the train and walked to Tallahassee and beat the train's arrival. Or at any rate, that is how the local legend goes.

The disturbances grew in all directions in the 1845 to 1860 period in Florida. There were more runaway slaves, more petty crimes, more money, more poverty, setting the classes apart. Only the upper class learned to read. The state's banks continued to contribute to periodic depressions and economic instability, and politically the Democrats and Republicans were deeply divided on most issues.

Governor Madison Perry, in office from 1857 to 1861, was a strong Democrat. He used his position to ready the state for secession from the United States with funds and militia prepared to fight. When the Legislature met just after the election of Abraham Lincoln as President of the United States in December 1860, there was deep concern in Florida to see a Republican in office. In January 1861 Florida hastily decided to leave the Union and help establish the Confederate States of America.

Many of Florida's finest early statesmen, her founders and thinkers, were set against secession. Former Gover-

Susan Bradford Eppes

nor Richard Keith Call, by then a senior statesman, was heart broken at Florida's rash action.

A privileged teen-aged girl, Susan Bradford, whose father owned a Leon County plantation, was allowed to accompany her father to the secession convention at the Capitol in Tallahassee. A huge crowd had assembled to witness the signing. She kept a journal with a detailed report of the meeting when Florida withdrew from the United States on January 11, 1861. She left this serious account of the affair:

"The stillness could almost be felt. One by one they came forward [to sign for secession].

When at length the names were all affixed, cheer after cheer rent the air; it was deafening. Our world seemed to have gone wild.

General Call is an old man now; and he is a strong Union man. Chancing to look toward him I saw that the tears were streaming down his face. Everybody cannot be suited and we are fairly launched on these new waters; may the voyage be a prosperous one".

Susan Bradford Eppes

Chapter Seven

The Civil War

The Early Years

The new nation, the Confederate States of America, made up of states which seceded from the United States, was formed in Mongomery, Alabama, in February 1861. Conflicts between the Confederate States and the government of the United States were not only over the right to own other humans as slaves but also the right of any state within the United States to withdraw from the Union, usually described as "states' rights". When Abraham Lincoln was inaugurated as President of the United States in March 1861 he clearly indicated that he was not an abolitionist, but he felt that the Union of states must remain as the central government of the United States and that no state could withdraw from it.

The first actual shooting, which took place before the establishment of the Confederate States, occurred in Pensacola at Fort Barrancas on January 6, 1861. Union guards posted there saw a group of Florida militiamen near the fort and a warning volley was fired to disperse them. A few days later, anticipating continued problems with local militiamen, the officer in charge of Fort Barrancas moved his soldiers and sailors to Fort Pickens, then unoccupied, but by reason of its location at the mouth of Pensacola harbor, more defensible and more important to the Union.

After a month of both sides attempting to reach a compromise between the breakaway states and the Union, the Confederate government, continuing the process of taking over Union military sites, demanded the surrender of Fort Sumter, located on a little island in the Charleston, South Carolina harbor. On April 12, 1861, Confederate artillery, apparently without orders from higher authority, started bombarding this fort, which surrendered the next day. The flag of the United States had been fired on, the Union and the Confederacy both started calling up troops, a total of eleven southern states had seceded from the Union, and the long and bloody Civil War started.

Teenagers Go to War

Will Denham, Confederate soldier from Monticello

Will Denham of Monticello was an eighteen year old student at the West Florida Seminary when he told his parents that he intended to enlist in the Confederate Army in June 1861.

"My son, my son," cried his mother. "Why must you do this? You have your education to finish, you have your parents to consider. Why, you are only a child!"

"Leave the lad alone to make a man's decision," said Will's father Andrew, who had arrived in Florida as a young man wearing a kilt from his native Scotland.

So Will went to war, was attached to a company sent
to attack Fort Pickens near Pensacola, and had one eye
shot out. He was medically discharged and returned
home where his family nursed him back to health.

At nineteen, half-blind and bored to death with being
a teenage hero to his friends and neighbors, he enlisted
again, this time in Florida's Company of Independent
Cavalry Volunteers. His outraged mother saw him off
with prayers and wonder at the folly of male children,
and he had his picture taken for her, the newest rage for
soldiers. Photography was only about as old as the state
of Florida.

Sergeant Will took part in the Battle of Olustee and
was later captured near Jacksonville by black Union
troops. In 1865, after being in prison, he was exchanged
and returned to Florida shortly before the Confederate
surrender.

Cracker cowboys of Florida, a drawing by Frederick Remington

Another story of two teenagers concerns a pair of brothers from the frontier cattle land of central Florida. Union and Confederate sympathisers lived there side by side, less interested in the issues of war than in fending off gangs of deserters and cattle rustlers. The atmosphere, rough and violent, affected the boys. They fought and wrestled every day when they were not involved in their heavy chores on the range.

Their scrapping and arguing continued until their mother vowed she'd throw them out to the alligators.

"Brother," said the older son one evening when they sat on the porch fighting mosquitoes instead of each other, "let's go to war."

"Why not," replied the younger one. "Ma and Pa can manage without us."

"Pa, we're going to war, real war where we get a uniform, a gun, and maybe some pay. We'll get conscripted anyhow, one side or the other. We'd be better off to volunteer."

"Which side?" asked Pa. "You'd be good fighters, but you'll never agree."

"I'll take the blue," said one.

"Then I'll take the gray," said the other.

The brothers enlisted, one on each side. They walked together to Gainesville where recruiters could be contacted.

They both came through the war without a wound or a badge of distinction. When they got home they took up the family scrapping again until they each got married and had a large brood of children who took up all their energy.

The Confederate Navy

The Confederacy consisted principally of agricultural states, with little manufacturing capacity to support a war. The Union states were larger in population and had both agriculture and manufacturing to support their military forces. In addition the Union Navy quickly established a blockade to prevent supplies from reaching the Confederacy. Some supplies came in but the blockade was generally effective.

The Confederacy as a weak sea power used armed cruiser raiders to destroy or capture Union merchant shipping. The most successful were the CSS Alabama, CSS Florida and CSS Shenandoah, which cruised foreign sea routes looking for United States merchant ships. None of these ships frequented Florida waters.

The superior Union Navy and ground troops captured Pensacola, Apalachicola, Cedar Key, Fernandina, Saint Augustine, and Jacksonville in 1862. Several of these ports changed sides periodically during the rest of the war, as troops were moved in and out. Key West remained in Union hands. Tampa was a blockaded port defended by various militia and volunteer companies until it was finally briefly occupied by Union forces in May 1864.

Confederate ship "Florida" destroys clipper ship, 1863

Nursing the Soldiers

When the Civil War began in 1861, one of the first concerns was taking care of the wounded soldiers. Since Florida troops were mostly sent to northern fronts, a hospital was needed in the fighting area. Richmond, Virginia, then the capital of the Confederacy, was chosen for an enormous medical center, Chimborazo, with five units. It was the largest hospital in the world, treating 76,000 patients during the war.

Howard's Grove, the Florida section of the hospital, was headed by Dr. Thomas Palmer of Monticello. The matron was Mrs. Mary Martha Reid, also of Monticello, the widow of Florida's territorial governor Robert R. Reid. Florida's unit had 150 beds.

At this period the only anesthesia for amputations and other painful surgery was whiskey. In all the units it was the matron's duty to control the whiskey. Sometimes the women had to fight to hold onto the keys that controlled this precious commodity. All the nurses were volunteers, and they lived hazardous lives.

Health problems on the home front were a challenge to other women in Florida. Some families opened their homes as hospitals to sick transient soldiers, and towns pitched in together when epidemics swept through.

The Confederate government had six hospitals in Florida with 515 beds. Private donations and the work of volunteer nurses were chiefly responsible for this little known work on the home front.

The Later Years

A great deal of the Civil War fighting in Florida consisted of raids and skirmishes, particularly in the Peace River region of central Florida. Settlements were burned, people captured, and local feuds flourished. Beef was captured for use by both Union and Confederate forces.

The major battle which occurred in Florida was at Olustee or Ocean Pond, near Lake City, in a Union effort to cut off the top of Florida to prevent supplies from reaching the Confederates to the north. Union forces consisting of both white and black units started from Jacksonville and followed the railroad line west toward Tallahassee. The armies were about evenly matched. The battle lasted for six hours on February 20, 1864, with Confederate casualties of 946 and Union casualties of 1,861. The Union troops withdrew. Confederate forces captured large amounts of military arms and supplies.

In September 1864 Union General Alexander Asboth moved out of Fort Barrancas in Pensacola with a raiding party of 700 mounted troops. They reached Marianna where the town was defended by about 150 youths and old men known as the "Cradle and Grave Company", plus some home guards and Confederate regulars on sick leave. After an uneven fight the town was looted but not burned. General Asboth was among the Union wounded.

Battle of Olustee

A historic battle took place in March 1865, when about 1,000 Union forces consisting of both black and white troops landed from fourteen Union naval vessels. The plan was to capture the port of St. Marks, then march north to sieze Tallahassee. The Union troops landed near the St. Marks lighthouse and marched up the east side of the St. Marks River. Finding the railroad bridge at St. Marks burned and the bridge at Newport dismantled, they moved on up the river bank to an area known as "Natural Bridge" where the river briefly goes underground allowing persons to walk across.

On the way, they passed a house where a sick-leave Confederate soldier was sitting on the front porch. The Yankees took him into custody, placed him in a wagon, and took him to Natural Bridge, where a relative of his was part of the Confederate defense. After the Union troops were defeated, they retreated to their ships, but dropped the sick Confederate off at his home to continue his recovery!

The defenders of Natural Bridge and Tallahassee consisted of youths called the "Baby Battalion", cadets and students at the West Florida Seminary in Tallahassee. They were aided by an assortment of older men, wounded Confederates, home guards, and any one else willing to fight. The Confederates numbered about 700, with a number of Seminary cadets being turned down because they did not have their parents' permission! A Tallahassee resident reported seeing three little boys, each carrying a gun, riding to the battle on one horse. Casualties were relatively light, three Confederates killed, twenty-three wounded, and twenty-one Union troops killed, eighty-nine wounded and thirty-eight missing in action.

Union forces repeatedly tried to destroy the Confederate salt works where sea salt was produced by evaporation. Up and down the long coastline such small units lay half-hidden by grass and palmettos. Salt was essential for the preservation of the beef from central Florida and other foods for the troops.

Confederate Salt Works, Gulf Coast, 1862

At the beginning of the Civil War, large numbers of northern Florida's young men, either members of local militia units or as volunteers, flocked into Confederate forces. Most of these troops were sent to northern battle-grounds rather than staying at home to defend their own state. It is estimated that about 15,000 white Floridians joined the Confederates, while around 1,200 white and 1,000 black Floridians joined the Union military. At least a third of the Confederates are believed to have lost their lives from combat or disease.

Surrender

The Confederate forces under General Robert E. Lee surrendered to Union General U. S. Grant at Appomattox Court House, Virginia on April 9, 1865. Other Confederate forces surrendered within a few days, and the Confederate army was totally disbanded by June 1865. After the Union capture of Richmond, the Confederate capital,

Chase of a blockade runner, 1864

and Lee's surrender, the civilian leaders of the southern states fled to safer territories.

Tallahassee, the only capital in the southern states not captured by Union forces, finally surrendered to Brigadier General Edward McCook on May 10, 1865. Demobilized southern troops began straggling home, facing a new life, new poverty, and a new culture, as a defeated nation, no longer a member of the United States. Since the Civil War had been fought chiefly within the Confederate states, that is where the worst destruction had taken place. The former slaves were uneducated, unemployed, sometimes still sympathetic, and sometime hostile toward their former masters. The South, after this defeat, was basically without government and money.

After a bloody and destructive period of warfare, Florida was now facing an even more tragic and difficult period of history, Reconstruction.

Chapter Eight

Reconstruction

In 1865 Florida's soldiers, both black and white, broken, wounded, sick, hungry, and defeated, returned, mostly on foot. One compassionate Yankee arranged for a wagon to bring home a load of exhausted Confederates from North Carolina.

Whatever money anyone had was in worthless Confederate bills. (Many Florida attics still have a box of them!) Fields were bare, houses out of repair or burned by raiding bands, many families were dead or had disappeared. There were no displays of flags or music, just quiet family celebrations, if the loved ones had survived the separation. A great body of family folk lore, often exaggerated, grew out of these memories in both races. The old system was gone, the Confederacy was defeated, and there was no Constitutional government in place.

Oh, sad black April of 1865! On the first day of the month, Florida's Governor John Milton made a heartsick speech to his friends and fellow officials and went home and blew his brains out.

On April 14, President Abraham Lincoln, attending a performance at a Washington theater, was shot and killed by actor John Wilkes Booth.

Confederate money

"O CAPTAIN! MY CAPTAIN!

O Captain! my Captain! our fearful trip is
done;
The ship has weathered every rack, the
prize we sought is won;
The port is near, the bells I hear, the
people all exulting,
While follow eyes the steady keel, the
vessel grim and daring:
But O Heart! heart! heart!
O the bleeding drops of red,
Where on the deck my Captain lies,
Fallen cold and dead."

In this poem Walt Whitman again cried out for the
entire nation at the grim terror that seized both North
and South.

One Confederate soldier, en route home, saw Old
Glory being shot at by a gang of hoodlums in front of a
Virginia courthouse. He risked his life to capture the flag
in the midst of the bullets. "It's mine again now, same as
the Confederate flag," he said. He brought it home as a
family treasure, a reminder of a death defying youthful
gesture to help restore his bleeding country.

Immediate action was needed. Florida was without a
governor, and the country was without a president. Vice
President Andrew Johnson took over as President, prom-
ising to follow the policies of Lincoln.

Since Florida had no Lieutenant Governor, Abraham
K. Allison, president of the senate, stepped in as acting
governor until elections could be held. With can-do energy, he was the man of the hour as he efficiently appointed committees to take care of the state emergency.
He set a date for the Assembly to convene to elect a
governor. It did not occur to him to wring his hands and
cry for help from Washington where Lincoln lay dead.

Allison dispatched five men to Washington to report

his actions. The Federal powers were enraged that Florida would presume to act intelligently and alone in the emergency. Before Allison could take a deep breath Federal troops had set in motion military occupation of Florida, and the acting Governor plus some other local leaders were clapped into jail.

Lincoln had been planning for postwar government in the South. His attitude was that the Union could not be broken and therefore the Union would bring the South back gently like erring brothers to work together for a stronger United States. This was carefully crafted, and Vice-President Johnson, as soon as he was sworn in, set out to implement Lincoln's agenda.

But there was a third element at work. Lincoln and his Congress had been at odds throughout the war. Now Congress declared that they would deal with the Reconstruction of the South and forget Lincoln and Johnson and their kindlier plan. An appointed Congressional committee said they'd deal with these defeated Confederates and bring them to their knees. They'd punish and punish until Lincoln and Johnson plus all the intelligent leaders in the South were dead and buried. It was a mean spirited operation according to the thinkers and writers of the day. Radical and militant Congressional leaders tried over and over to impeach President Johnson for his attempts to deal fairly with the South.

By December 1865 Florida had a provisional government in place, made up partly of pardoned former leaders. Not all people were eligible for pardons, but President Johnson issued them to former leaders of good standing who were needed to stabilize Florida's future.

William Marvin, a Floridian, a Union sympathiser, and a moderate man, was appointed governor. His was a difficult job, but he steered the Tallahassee government between the reality of the military presence and the destroyed society around him. The first step toward reunion was to ratify the Thirteenth Amendment to the United States Constitution, which abolished slavery. The

Florida Assembly "annulled" secession and accepted the emancipation of slaves.

Florida's Most Famous Prisoner

Meantime the assassination of Abraham Lincoln by actor John Wilkes Booth was quickly found to be a part of a plot involving a number of people who were quickly brought to justice. Some were hanged and others imprisoned. When Booth fired the fatal shot he leaped from the presidential box onto the stage, intending to make a getaway on his waiting horse, but he broke his leg in the jump.

His companion in the alleyway got him onto the horse and they rode away through Maryland. There the companion took him to the home and office of Dr. Samuel Mudd for medical help. The question was, was Dr. Mudd a part of the plot, set up to be a helper to Booth, the murderer? Dr. Mudd took care of the injured man, but denied that he had ever seen him before. That proved to be untrue.

Finally Dr. Mudd was formally accused and tried by a military court as part of the conspiracy to kill the President. There was great doubt that he was guilty as charged, but there were unanswered questions. Dr. Mudd was convicted by the court and imprisoned at Fort Jefferson on Dry Tortugas, the outermost of the Florida Keys.

It was a terrible hell-hole of a place. Mudd's friends and relatives tried without ceasing to have him pardoned and released. Finally, a disaster saved the doctor. Yellow fever broke out among the prisoners and Union soldiers stationed there. Dr. Mudd's medical skill came to his help. He worked brilliantly and tirelessly, saving many lives, but he was still a prisoner.

His faithful wife continued to work for his release. She tried once more to see President Andrew Johnson who was soon to leave office. Johnson heard her story to the end. One of his last acts in office was to grant a pardon to

Dr. Samuel Mudd who returned to Maryland and his family and his medical practice.

Efforts to Cope

The Freedmen's Bureau was established by the Federal government to help the freed slaves adjust to the new order. "Carpetbaggers", a loose term meaning northerners who came south to help or hinder, bearing their belongings in carpet cloth satchels, arrived in droves. Many stayed to settle in Florida.

There were infighting groups such as the Ku Klux Klan, at first a social club, which later grew into a vicious vigilante group to control perceived disorders among freed slaves. "Black Codes" were drawn up in with the idea of preserving the old order, and Black Brotherhoods were established for mutual support and self protection of former slaves.

In spite of this tension there was little actual racial violence. Most of the former slaves, having no place else to go, went back to plantations where various work plans were arranged individually, but the problems of hordes of lost or unemployed freedmen and newly-poor white planters were not solved for generations.

An old Florida cabin home

100

By 1868 a new Constitution was adopted in Florida by a convention which also ratified the Federal Fourteenth Amendment, affirming the equal rights of citizenship to adult males of all races. This was not done without some bitter political fighting. Some delegates boycotted the convention and a breakaway group wrote a second constitution in Monticello. Matters were finally settled in this assembly of blacks, whites, ex-slaves, ex-planters, carpetbaggers, Union representatives and a few men of courage and intelligence from all sides who tried to establish a fair government for the state. Florida was restored to the Union on July 4, 1868.

Two outstanding black men emerged from this period of government. Jonathan Gibbs, a well educated man from Philadelphia, a member of the 1868 Florida Constitutional Convention, was appointed Secretary of State. His main interest was in the education of all Florida citizens so, in 1873, after serving for five years as Secretary of State, he became the state Superintendant of Public Instruction until his death in 1874.

Josiah T. Walls, a self-educated northern black man was elected to the United States House of Representatives. Brought up in Virginia, Walls had a moderate attitude as a member of the 1868 Convention. He held numerous state positions prior to his election to Congress in 1870 in a bitter race. It was 1874 before he was seated in that body.

Walls became a newspaper editor, teacher, a model farmer, and a popular citizen. He too is chiefly remembered for his fight for black education. He successfully arranged for a 90,000 acre land grant to support the Florida Normal College, now Florida Agricultural and Mechanical University, better known as FAMU.

Florida's Republican Reconstruction was officially over in 1876. But Florida's troubles with poverty, racial discrimination, lack of schools, and labor problems were not settled until great changes came with the passage of the Civil Rights Act of 1964.

Chapter Nine

Schools and Race Relations

The Earliest Schooling

When the first Indians came into Florida there was tribal teaching for children. How else could the race survive? They needed to know how to build a fire or shelter, how to kill and prepare game, how to cook, plant, and weave, or tan skins. They needed to know how to remember family stories and customs, and how to live with others. Probably special persons were designated to teach groups.

When the Spanish came in the sixteenth century with their shiploads of would-be colonists, among the women and children who accompanied the fighting men, someone evidently gathered the children around and taught them to read and write a few Spanish letters. When the Spanish settled St. Augustine they had real schools, taught by the priests and lay brothers of the Church. The oldest school house in America still stands in St. Augustine.

Later on when the Missions began to spread over north Florida, schools were a part of the picture. Many Indians learned to read and write Spanish and to practice useful trades. Later the Spanish in St. Augustine set up an English language school for children. The only catch was that a student had to know how to read and write Spanish before he could enroll. This was an effort to train Spanish leaders in an area where most people spoke English.

When the British came to govern Florida (1763-1783) they also had children to educate. When the Anglican clergy replaced the Roman Catholics the sounds of learning were in English from the Catechism in the Book of Common Prayer, instead of the Roman Catechism. The Church was always in the forefront teaching children to read so the holy words would survive. Some families had Bibles from which the children were taught to read.

The American Revolution occurred during Florida's British period, flooding the state with Loyalists who left the American colonies. Many of these were wealthy and well educated and their children continued their learning with home schools or church classes. They no doubt brought with them their reading books the *New England Primer* and the *Hornbook* for the beginners. A hornbook was actually a square with a handle with the alphabet and numbers printed on each side. Sometimes they were made of horn, but usually were wooden with painted letters.

Slow Progress

When Florida became a Territory of the United States, the Federal government reserved lands for schools, although it was a long time before any were built. The idea of education was spelled out in Florida's first Constitution. Tracts of land were designated for the support of two "normal schools" for higher education, one east and one west of the Suwannee River. Nothing was proposed for elementary schooling.

There were various efforts to teach children using private academies, tutors, neighborhood schools, and home teaching, but only for white children. In 1831 the Florida Education Society was formed in Tallahassee, and branches were organized in other towns. Although this organization tried to set up some schools, there were no state funds and the schools did not succeed.

In 1851 the West Florida Seminary was finally opened,

which helped educate teachers. Built on the site of the present Florida State University, it soon opened its doors to women. By 1860 the school gave Bachelor of Arts degrees, and there were 200 students enrolled.

Theories and Ideas for Schools

Leaders of the day listened to theories and considered how best to educate the children; there was a lot of talk but no clear plan to follow. One educated physician, father of fourteen children, was determined to give his children a good education, boys and girls alike. In those antebellum days, a "good" education meant classic subjects, including Greek and Latin. These children's schooling began at age five with each child, boy or girl, using a tutor or a willing relative to teach reading, spelling, mathematics, history, geography and the classics. Writing was especially important in those days when there were no computers or typewriters and all records and communications had to be transcribed in readable handwriting.

One room school and women's clubhouse, Coconut Grove, 1889

Each child had to memorize a chapter in the Bible to be recited to their stern father every Sunday. This routine kept up until the child was twelve years old. At that point the boys were put to work in the fields.

The Civil War interrupted this home educational plan, but while slavery existed the boys worked side by side with the slaves until they were eighteen. After the war when labor was a serious problem, the sons kept the plantation labor going. Any money earned was used for college.

All the sons became college graduates to go on into the world as doctors, teachers, lawyers, and professional men in other fields.

Nor did the girls escape this rigorous education. At twelve they began to work in the dairy, the house, the kitchen, the weaving room, and in the care of the sick. At eighteen, before they were married, they each had a year of higher education at finishing school or normal school.

First School System Mandated for All

In 1849 Florida's first state school system was set up by law with a state superintendant, local school boards, trustees, and authorized funds. Children had to attend for a minimum of three months a year. The framework was set, but there was a slow start for functioning schools throughout the state. And then the war intervened in 1861.

There was violent opposition to even considering schools for black children. In Virginia, Mrs. Margaret Douglas, an upper class white woman, set up a school for freedmen's children in her home. She was arrested and imprisoned for this daring "crime" which brought forth many derogatory editorials in contemporary newspapers. Mrs. Douglas, who had friends and relatives among the north Florida gentry, was the subject of much gossip.

Black education began at the end of the Civil War

Florida pioneers

when the slaves were freed. Even before state laws could be enacted for a black school system, benevolent societies and churches set up free schools for them. In 1866 black education became legal and official in Florida, and by the end of that year there were sixty-five elementary schools for black children, mostly in one room buildings.

There was strict segregation, but soon laws decreed that white and black schools should have equal assets. They were not equal, in spite of the laws. The black schools had poor buildings, inadequate books and supplies, less educated and lower paid teachers, and poor supervision from state officials.

The white community in that poverty stricken Reconstruction period had so many problems of their own that there was little interest in the black schools, and white schools of this turn of the century period were not very well equipped either. Today Florida has 1,424 elementary public schools and 365 high schools, all free and integrated.

After the Supreme Court of the United States made the decision in 1954 that school segregation was unconstitutional, Dade County was the first Florida school district to comply. Florida was the first of all the Southern states in school integration.

Florida's largest state universities, Florida State University, the University of Florida, and Florida Agricultural and Mechanical University, as well as a number of smaller universities and colleges, community colleges and specialized institutions now provide higher education for all qualified students.

Mary McLeod Bethune's Miracle School

Mary McLeod Bethune

Florida's educational story is filled with names of dedicated people who worked for better schools for both whites and blacks, but none equals perky, vibrant, Mary McLeod Bethune who established Bethune College at Daytona Beach in 1904. Her assets to begin this school were brains, faith, a will of iron, and $1.50 in cash.

The daughter of ex-slaves, Mary McLeod learned to read in a missionary church school. She walked five miles, twice a day, to reach her school. She was such an eager student that she won a scholarship to Scotia Seminary in North Carolina and finally to Moody Bible Institute in Chicago. Her ambition was to be a foreign missionary. Instead she ended up in Daytona. The need for a school there was so great she knew this was the place she was meant to be.

She found a vacant shack which she rented for eleven dollars a month, with the promise to pay later, and began a speaking career in local churches and schools or wherever she could pass the hat. She was a gifted speaker with a mission.

Duval County school bus, 1898

With a child to support (her husband had soon deserted them) in October 1904 she opened her miracle school with six pupils. The tuition was fifty cents a week. Two years later the school had 250 pupils! Benefactors, white and black, always appeared in the nick of time. She operated on faith, she said.

By 1906 she had a school plant with space, books, electricity and running water. In 1909 Cookman Institute in Jacksonville merged with Bethune to become Bethune-Cookman College in Daytona Beach. It became well endowed from wealthy residents of Florida.

Finally someone gave her a trip to Europe where she even had tea with royalty. President Franklin D. Roosevelt invited Mrs. Bethune to the White House where she was appointed a special advisor to the President and to other important positions where her assertive intelligence worked wonders for black children for the rest of her life.

Mrs. Triplett and Her Happy Story

Ethel Triplett, an eighty-five year old black matriarch from rural Wakulla County tells of her experiences at school in the early 1900's.

"This is a happy story," she says." I loved my school. That little building is still standing, but it isn't a school now. No, I didn't envy the white schools. There weren't any near us. I never saw one in those days," she laughs.

"We went to school three months a year, and we shared reading books. We'd stand in line in front of the teacher to read. When I'd finish my part I'd pass the book on to the next person. My great-grandchildren have a lot more books than we did."

"Spelling was the same. We'd stand up in a row to spell, and we used the blackboard a lot for words and arithmetic. When we had paper we used ink bottles and pens so we could learn to write neatly."

"Yes, we had outdoor privies for toilets, and we had a well and a water bucket and a pot bellied stove. And we got switched when we were bad, but we had fun at school. There was a sinkhole behind the school where we could hide at recess and dance and sing. On Friday afternoons we'd have recitations and invite our parents to come."

"No snacks or lunches were provided. We brought our dinners in little lard buckets and ate whatever we had to spare from home. Sometimes we didn't have anything, and on those days we didn't eat unless somebody shared. We did a lot of sharing in our community."

Mrs. Triplett went on to say that all of her children became college graduates and teachers. Her many descendants go to Florida's integrated schools. Was that a hard transition? Mrs. Triplett tells of the joyful gathering of whites and blacks in the big county high school gymnasium when the change was made.

"I sat on the front row. Whites and blacks all mixed in together in this beautiful school with nice bathrooms and a library and good lights and nobody mad. We were all happy together."

Turbulent Racial Changes

There were other unfair social issues beyond the segregation of schools. Mrs. Triplett's story was one of the few happy ones.

In the post Reconstruction era when the freed slaves and their descendants learned to read they were more and more discontented with their lot. In 1954 Florida had segregated schools, restaurants, movies, hospitals, restrooms, and even drinking fountains. On trains African-Americans had to ride in separate cars and use separate waiting rooms, and buses required all blacks to ride in the rear.

African-American leaders, especially the Reverend Martin Luther King, Jr. encouraged a non-violent struggle to give equal rights to his people. Although Dr. King was not a Floridian, he and his close friend the Reverend C. K. Steele, pastor of Tallahassee's Bethel Baptist Church, conferred often about the segregation problems in Florida.

In May 1956 two students from Florida A. and M. University, FAMU, were jailed for sitting down in the front seats of a city bus! They had been ordered to the back of the bus where there were no empty seats. When they asked to have their fares refunded, the driver called the police. This incident set off a local bus boycott which lasted eighteen months, until the U.S. Supreme Court ruled that public facilities, such as buses, could not be segregated.

The Reverend C. K. Steele was the leader of this civil rights non-violent struggle, and a statue honoring him stands in front of the Tallahassee bus station today. The bus boycott in Tallahassee affected the entire state for soon there was a wave of sit-ins at lunch counters and theaters. Hundreds of FAMU students were arrested, more than the jail could hold. It was a stirring time in Florida, but finally the fights, tear gas, burning crosses, and sit-ins had a peaceful outcome. The fair minded attitude of Governors Leroy Collins and Reubin Askew had a calming effect during the crisis.

By the end of the 1960's school integration was complete, people could sit where they wished, swim in public pools, eat at any restaurant, and use the hospitals and libraries, without regard to race or color. The Civil Rights Act of 1964 was hailed as a major step in American democracy.

Rev. C.K. Steele spearheads bus integration in Tallahassee

Chapter Ten

Railroads, Real Estate and Tourists

Flagler, Plant, Disston, and Collier. These are some of the names that spell the new development of Florida. Big time railroads, elegant hotels, and rich tourists added up to a new civilization in old Florida's failed and debt ridden post Reconstruction economy.

The climate appealed so much to the sick and wealthy that it was said that Floridians lived on sweet potatoes and consumptive Yankees! Around 1876 investors looked at orange groves, timber, and idle lands and reached for their checkbooks.

1880's railroad

Flagler

Standard Oil's Henry M. Flagler came to Jacksonville in his private railroad car in 1878, making his way on down to St. Augustine by ferry and narrow gauge railroad. He decided that St. Augustine needed an elegant hotel and better transportation. He missed his fancy special car which could travel no further south than Jacksonville.

Flagler built in St. Augustine the finest hotel ever seen in Florida, attracting the famous and fashionable from all over the world. At the same time he built a railroad bridge across the St. Johns River and installed a new railroad south for his comfort. He continued opening up the east coast with hotels and railroads all the way to Fort Dallas, now Miami, in 1896.

When Flagler was seventy-four years old he began to extend his railroad to Key West. This amazing over-the-water bridge took 400,000 workmen years to construct. In 1912, Flagler, now eighty-two, rode in his precious private car to the tip of Florida. Flagler was wealthy beyond belief and a massive land owner, having been given 8,000 acres of state land for every mile of rails he constructed.

Disston

Hamilton Disston, a Philadelphia saw manufacturer, came to Florida on Flagler's train in 1881, to do some fishing. He saw an overlooked possibility: why not drain the wetlands? He formed a company which offered to drain Florida's vast swamps in exchange for half of the land drained. He agreed to buy 4,000,000 acres of over-flowed land for twenty-five cents an acre which gave the state $1,000,000 to pay off bonded debts.

Disston used dredges to build canals and deepen rivers so that steamboats could come into the Caloosahatchee River near Fort Myers and travel to Lake Okeechobee and then up the Kissimmee River. He gave

land on which the government set up an agricultural
experiment station and started Florida's first sugar mills.
Disston finally went broke and killed himself in 1896.

Plant

Meantime Henry B. Plant had come to Florida to buy
up bankrupt railroads. Beginning in Tampa, he got 4,000
acres of state land for each mile constructed. He wanted
a magnificant hotel too, so he constructed the landmark
Tampa Bay Hotel in 1891, now part of the University of
Tampa.

During the Spanish American War, this hotel was the
headquarters of the military command. Plant himself
helped run the waterfront by moving troops, including
Teddy Roosevelt's Rough Riders.

Collier

Barron Collier, who had made a fortune on street car
advertising in New York, spent his money on Florida
land. He became fascinated with the Everglades in 1911.
When the state tried to build a highway across the
Everglades and failed, Collier offered to finish it. He did,
and the Tamiami Trail was opened in 1926. Collier County
is named for this risk-taking entrepreneur.

Building the Tamiami Trail

Merrick

One of the last of the early developers was not a traditional rich financier. George Merrick was a preacher's son from old Coconut Grove. He saw that there was no planned community in Florida where middle class people could live in comfort, not like the mansion society that was now moving into Palm Beach and other fashionable playgrounds for the rich. Merrick established and developed the city of Coral Gables and founded the University of Miami in 1926, on the eve of the Great Depression. Like the other big developers he went bankrupt.

However, Merrick was something of a home town boy. He did not lose his faith in Florida, but instead he and his wife stuck it out and opened a little fishing camp in the keys until the economy improved and he could move back to Coral Gables and reopen his real estate business.

Fisher

Carl Fisher, who built roads and bridges and fortunes, came to Miami in 1913. He looked across the span of water that separated Miami and the jewel of a tropical island, Miami Beach, and decided to build a bridge to connect them. With his associate John Collins, they not only built a splendid causeway but, needing more land, pumped up sand from the bay bottom and built islands for beautiful homes.

Fisher wrapped up his Florida fame by creating the Dixie Highway, a road that would get the new automobile public from the Midwest down to the wonderland of South Florida, where lots were for sale.

Further Growth

There were scores of other successful promoters of Florida whose names are still remembered such as John Stetson, General Henry Sanford, Henry DeLand, D. P. Davis, and Alfred I. duPont.

In 1926 the Florida real estate boom exploded. In the same year Miami was almost destroyed by a killer hurricane, but Florida's growth didn't stop. A new generation of people who had lost their jobs in the Great Depression of the 1930's brought their "Tin Lizzies" down the Dixie Highway to warmer weather carrying tents, canned food, and camping equipment. They were called "tin can tourists". It became a poor people's Florida as well as a rich playground.

One of the big daily events of this new railroad land was to watch the trains come in and go, a free sport for all ages. Who's arriving? And why? The railroad station was the social center of the town for mail, gossip, and news. Telegraphers in each station talked to each other up and down the lines, not only about train business but also about local events.

When airports slowly became the order of the day, people swarmed to see what was happening there. The first scheduled airline in the U. S. flew passengers and cargo from St. Petersburg to Tampa in 1914. Pan American Airlines developed from a merger of small airlines under the leadership of Juan Trippe. Its seaplane terminal at Coconut Grove's Dinner Key had a giant globe in the center of the ground floor that turned slowly for children and grownups to watch and wish on.

Dinner Key, where seaplanes were launched into the water, provided passenger service to the West Indies and Central and South America. A small island close to shore in the center of Coconut Grove, Dinner Key got its quaint name from the fact that pioneers there liked to take their Sunday dinners in picnic baskets out to the little key in their boats.

The flat terrain and mild climate made Florida a perfect site for aviation. World War I hero, Eddie Rickenbacker founded Eastern Airlines, and his first mail route brought these planes to Florida where they became a familiar sight all over the state. Little boys, and little girls too, grew up fascinated with watching planes land and take off at local airports. Here is a copy of an actual post card to an air minded Florida boy who had answered an advertisement in a magazine.

••••

Feb. 20, 1928

Dear Sir;-

We have your coupon asking for information about our Aviation Course, but as you are just 12, we are asking that you wait for a few years, as we do not enroll students that young. At a later date, however, we shall be glad to hear from you again, and will send you the literature that you ask for.

Thanking you for your inquiry, and hoping to hear from you again, we remain
          Yours very truly,
          SWEENEY AVIATION SCHOOL"
••••

Chapter Eleven

Florida and Cuba

Cuban Cigars

Florida and Spanish Cuba have had a close connection for 300 or so years. Most of the Spanish conquerors of Florida set out from Cuba to claim and explore the mysterious finger of land to the north.

Cuba's greatest products have always been sugar and tobacco. Handmade Havana cigars were traditional world treasures, skillfully made by trained workers. Sugar and the excellent rums made from sugar cane were both in demand in the rest of the world. The cane and tobacco fields kept poor uneducated laborers in slave-like conditions, causing constant unrest and discontent with the rule of Spain. Leaders rose up from the masses to overthrow the Spanish government, and civil war went on for years. The Cubans looked with envy at the United States, wanting the same freedom and independence.

The political disorder in Cuba in the nineteenth century caused some of the cigar makers to move their factories to nearby Key West, but it was too close to Cuba and the workers brought their rebellious spirit with them. One of the leading manufacturers, Don Vincente Martinez Ybor, decided to move his cigar factory and workers to yet another location.

In 1885 Tampa was a small isolated country town, but it was expecting the railroad to come soon and bring the world to its doorstep. Señor Ybor chose beautiful cheap land several miles from Tampa and set up a factory and housing for employees there, naming the location Ybor City. Other cigar manufacturers soon followed.

Ybor City and New Ideas

Ybor City, which eventually became part of Tampa, was a unique Florida town, European in flavor and sophisticated in its manners and tastes. It was a melting pot of Cubans, Italians, Spanish, Africans, and a few Florida "crackers". The cigar makers were a proud group, feeling a bit superior with their skills, an attitude that led to frequent strikes against management.

Nowhere else in America, then or now, did workers pay readers or "lectors" to read aloud to them while they worked. Seated at long tables, rolling tobacco into cigars, the workers chose the lector and what was to be read and paid his wages.

Lector reading to cigar workers, Ybor City 1929

Each day the workers had the day's local news, international news, Cuban news, and a few chapters of a novel read to them. The readings were usually radical in nature, translated from many sources by the lector. For the most part management was unaware that revolutionary material was being read to the employees hour after hour in the cigar factories.

The cigar makers became an educated group, full of advanced and stirring ideas. Factory owners finally realized that for decades their workrooms had been training grounds for exotic political thinking and action. In 1931 the system of lectors was outlawed as being revolutionary. No more teaching and learning on the job. So what was the result? The workers went on strike, the only time on record that Florida workers struck for a cultural cause!

A Cooperative Town

Other unusual features of Ybor City were its mutual aid societies which were actually social clubs. At their elegant meeting halls they had dances, band concerts, operas, plays, libraries, and sports. The only appearance the famous singer Enrico Caruso ever made in Florida was at one of Ybor City's cigar makers' clubs. There were five major clubs in the town around the turn of the century. The clubs were not rivals, and there was no racial segregation until the state government prohibited integration, after which the Afro-Cubans set up their own club.

Perhaps the most interesting of all the Ybor City experiments was the cooperative medical venture. Yellow fever and tuberculosis were constant perils, and the clubs cooperated in building clinics and two hospitals, bringing in trained medical personel. The county medical society bitterly fought these successful ventures for the cigar workers and their families, who were getting the best of care at very low cost. Jealous Tampa physicians barred the Ybor City doctors and nurses from practicing in Tampa hospitals.

Meantime in Cuba the friends and relatives of the Florida Cubans continued to fight against the rule of Spain and received help from the Florida groups. One of Cuba's most honored rebel heroes, Jose Marti, spent a great deal of his time in Ybor City, calling it his second home, before he died in battle in the Cuban War for Independence in 1895.

The Spanish American War

United States troops were stationed in Florida, especially in Tampa, in 1898, for there was growing tension about the Cuban situation. The U.S. Battleship *Maine* was sent to Cuba to stand by if there should be trouble between Spain and the United States. Trouble came: somebody blew up the *Maine*, killing 260 Americans.

Tampa in the Spanish American War, 1898

Saber tooth tigers were once at home in Florida

*Football rivals - Florida State University
And University of Miami*

FAMU's Marching 100

Dancers at Florida State University

Sunshine Skyway - St. Petersburg and Bradenton

Florida Gold

Miami Beach Gold Coast

Capital Complex, Tallahassee

Modern Seminole family

West Coast sport fishing

Hurricane Andrew, damage and survivors

Nobody knew who set off the explosion. Florida was outraged along with the rest of the country, and newspapers fanned emotions with hot headlines. The survivors of the explosion were brought to Tampa, and the United States declared war on Spain.

The Spanish-American War was a brief one, lasting from April to August 1898. While the U.S. was fighting Spain so were the rebellious Cubans who had tried to be rid of Spanish rule for so long. When peace came Cuba did not want the North Americans to claim the total glory. The U.S. made no effort to seize Cuba although she did acquire the Philippines and Puerto Rico.

The U.S. gave aid to Cuba and withdrew her troops. Cuba was independent of Spain at last, and America was now at peace with the new democratic neighbor.

New Relations With Cuba

That situation did not last forever. A series of dictators, ending with the takeover of Cuba by Communist Fidel Castro in 1959, destroyed good relations. Castro's close ties to the Soviet Union posed a threat to the security of the United States.

Many Cubans fled, especially to Miami, from Castro's Communist Cuba. In 1961 Cuban rebel refugees and American sympathisers invaded the south coast of Cuba at the Bay of Pigs. President Kennedy authorized the invasion but decided at the last minute not to give air cover and naval support. The invaders expected the Cubans to rise up in revolt in protest to Castro, but they did not. It was a terrible defeat for U.S. policy, and an uneasy time for Florida, still not forgotten by Florida's Cuban exiles. There are over a million Cubans living in Florida today.

Florida was frightened again with the Cuban missile crisis in 1962. Soviet technicians, planes, equipment and missiles arrived in Cuba, with more on the way at sea. A missile attack on Florida could occur in minutes.

Cuban refugees, 1961

A tug of war literally took place, with U.S. naval and air forces deployed for possible combat. The missiles were finally removed after mutual threats, sea quarantine, and diplomatic efforts.

In 1980 Castro suddenly decided to open the doors of his prisons and mental institutions and deport thousands of inmates along with some dissatisfied citizens to Florida. This gambit, called the Mariel Boat Lift, moved some of Castro's problems to Miami. There was already a large Cuban community in Dade County, so many refugees found family support, and others were assimilated.

South Florida has accepted vast numbers of Haitian political refugees as well. Today "Little Havana" and "Little Haiti" have changed the face and the language of old Miami. Even some of the schools are taught in Spanish for the Cubans and French for the Haitians.

Chapter Twelve

World War II and Its Times

World War II

On Sunday, December 7, 1941, some young people went sailing in their small boats from the dock in Coconut Grove. They met for a picnic lunch on Key Biscayne, then a wild jungle island, now a fashionable resort.

It was a memorable day, not only for the sailing party, but for the world. When they tied up their boats at sunset stunning news was garbled out over a radio on the dock: Pearl Harbor had been bombed by the Japanese. Florida was plunged into World War II. The pleasure craft were put in storage as young people joined the forces. Some never came back. Florida's east coast port

World War II tanker burning off Hobe Sound

cities became Navy ship centers. Coastal areas, especially on the Atlantic, were blacked out at night for there were enemy submarines sneaking under the water. People grew victory gardens, had rationed gasoline, food, and clothing. The whole state turned its attention to the Red Cross, United Services Organization (USO), and other groups to help the troops. Interior Florida was soon filled with new Army and Air Corps bases and flying fields where the climate and terrain offered ideal conditions.

Pensacola, the site of the Navy's oldest flight training center, was stretched to bursting. All Navy fliers trained at Pensacola at one time or another not only during World War II, but also for the Korea, Vietnam, and Desert Storm conflicts. Today, at the Pensacola Naval Air Station there is a museum with a specimen of every United States Navy plane ever flown. This is considered the largest and most comprehensive display of naval flying equipment in the world, constructed for Floridians and people from all over the globe.

World War II Navy dive bombers over Miami, 1941

Women Take Part in War, and a Special Florida Heroine

Women served in many capacities in the military. In World War II when women's services became more common Florida women worked as nurses, enlisted personnel, and officers, in all branches of the service. One of Florida's distinguished fliers was Jacqueline Cochran, who came, as she said, "from the sawdust trail". She grew up in deep poverty in Panhandle Florida sawmill towns.

Jacqueline Cochran learned to read from the letters she saw on the railroad boxcars that ran past her door. She didn't know exactly how old she was nor her real name. She was probably born about 1918, a mysterious foster child, who was unhappy with her lot.

Jacqueline Cochran, aviator

She tried school (nobody cared if she went), but she got into such a fracas with the teacher the first day that she was expelled. She spent the year roaming the woods, fishing, and learning what she could do to survive in the saw mill and turpentine country where she lived. Next year she tried school again, and this time a sympathetic teacher helped this little girl to read and write and to seek the best in her cruel world. The teacher also discovered that Jackie was extra bright and gave her a boost in self confidence. This was her one year of schooling. She had to work.

In her autobiography *Stars At Noon*, Jacqueline Cochran tells of the incredibly poor and unloved child who walked down the sawdust road to such adventures as living with Gypsies, following the circus, and working for sick neighbors. Finally, in about 1926, her foster family moved to Georgia seeking better work. In Columbus, Georgia, Jackie got her first paying job, in a cotton mill for six cents an hour on a twelve hour shift. She believes she was about eight years old. She was a good worker and soon advanced in pay and responsibility. When a strike in the mill stopped all work she went to work in a beauty parlor as the lowliest employee.

Jackie Cochran was on a roller coaster for success. By the time she was fourteen she went to Montgomery, Alabama, where she learned more about the beauty business and was inspired to enroll in a nursing school. People in the community were kind to her, and she learned to cook, sew, keep house, and make friends. She became a reader, avid for books.

After finishing nurses training she moved back to Florida to help her people on sawdust road, but eventually went back into the beauty business. In her own little Ford car she drove to New York City where she worked in fashionable Fifth Avenue beauty shops. She was still a teenager, according to her own story, and her work took her to elegant salons in Palm Beach and Miami in the winter.

A man she met at a party encouraged her to try flying. He was Floyd Odlum, who eventually became her husband. Jackie took a three week vacation and went out to Long Island to enroll in a flying school. She was a natural flyer, and soon became not only a pilot, but a famous one.

In 1938 she was awarded the General "Billy" Mitchell Award as the American pilot who made the greatest individual contribution to aviation with her many prizes for risk taking and speed flying. Naturally she became involved in World War II aviation. She was called to be a ferry pilot, taking war planes to England. When America entered the war in 1941 President Franklin D. Roosevelt asked her to be the head of the WASPs (Women's Airforce Service Pilots) where she trained more women for vital service to their country.

Her flying continued into the jet age. She was a test pilot, a veteran race winner, bemedalled, honored and famous, a friend of Presidents and royalty. In 1953 she received her highest flying honor, the International Flying Organization's gold medal for outstanding accomplishment for all pilots. Her life of adventure took her around the world, many times, to confer with government heads and to see international post-war history in the making.

In her biography she wrote a message for Florida's young people. "My story went from sawdust to stardust....my message for America's youth is to flex your mental muscles and get cracking on your own power."

Modern Florida Indians

What happened to the Indians who hid and refused to be deported to Oklahoma? Today there are an estimated 36,000 Floridians who claim to be Indians, living in cities or on reservations. All Indians have had full citizenship since 1924.

In 1845, when Florida became a state, land was reserved at Big Cypress, Brighton, Hollywood, and Immokalee for the Seminoles who refused to leave Florida. There they have their own churches and schools, and govern and support themselves in various enterprises. At Big Cypress the Seminole Indians run a celebrated bingo hall, a major tourist attraction.

Related to the Seminoles, but different in language and religion, is the Miccosukee tribe, which once lived in Leon and Jefferson Counties. When U. S. Troops tried to capture and remove the Miccosukees, they quietly slipped down the Florida peninsula and eased into the Everglades, making a new home in the grass, water, and hammocks. Nobody could find them, and they held on to their identity in religion and language. They did not move to a reservation.

Over the years, many Americans, ashamed of the treatment of the Indians, tried to help them with gifts of land and medical assistance. During the Great Depression the Indians suffered dreadfully as private donations dried up and government funds vanished.

Deaconess Harriet Bedell

In 1933 Harriet Bedell, a newly retired deaconess in the Episcopal Church who had ministered to Indians in Alaska and Oklahoma, visited friends in Miami. For entertainment, her hostess took her to visit a tourist attraction, an Indian village. The Indians that Deaconess Bedell saw that day were shy Miccosukees in native dress, fenced in as curiosities on view like wild animals, for the paying public. The deaconess was horrified. She realized the shame they must feel to be exhibited in this degrading way to make a little money to survive. She tried to speak to them, but they did not respond. She made up her mind on the spot that she would devote the rest of her life to helping these Indians.

All she had was her meagre retired pay, but she

Deasoness Harriet Bedell with Chief Ingram Billie and family

managed to rent a little cabin near the Indians, and a friend gave her an old Model A Ford. She had never driven a car, but she learned at age fifty-four and began driving her way through the Everglades with love, food, and medical help for the Miccosukees.

They were hurting with hunger and poverty so she taught the women to sew and helped them sell their handicrafts. She learned their language and loved them for themselves. She got government and private aid but never tried to convert them to her religion. In 1962 she helped them to gain tribal status and 200,000 acres of Everglades where they could govern themselves, have their own school and control their own hunting and fishing areas. She saw to it that they were not displaced from their lands when the Everglades National Park was built.

She died at age eighty-five, a beloved and not very well known Florida heroine, a legend among the Miccosukee Indians today.

Disneyworld

Florida's history is not all wars and military might. It has always had a streak of frolic and fun in the sun, beaches, bathing beauties, and amusement parks to lure the tourists. A part of post World War II Florida is Disneyworld.

In 1962 Walt Disney began his highly publicized theme park, starting with the fantasy Magic Kingdom and expanding into Epcot Center and Disney MGM Studios. This enormous project was built on 27,000 acres of what was prized rural land only a few years before.

Orlando is a center for tourism that staggers central Florida, for Disneyworld has been the hub for many additional tourist attractions. The Orlando International Airport is the seventeenth busiest airport in the world, with 230,000 visitors a week pouring into the area in 1992. Information on Disneyworld is readily available in reliable guide books, (not written by Mickey and Minnie Mouse as one little boy believed!).

State Parks

Florida has preserved much of her physical and ethnic history in 113 state parks located throughout the state. Some feature museums, hiking trails, camping, canoeing, swimming, surfing, diving, fishing, whatever is possible in that special spot. If you want to see an Indian mound or go snorkeling, one of the parks will provide this feature. The entrance fees are modest. The Department of Natural Resources in Tallahassee has a free guidebook for all state parks. (Write to DNR, Div. of Recreation and Parks, 3900 Commonwealth Blvd. Tallahassee, FL 32399-3000)

Space

Once there were Indian mounds soaring over the flat lands of Florida. Today on Cape Canaveral and Merritt

Island on Florida's east coast near the Indian River the horizon is heightened by the sight of giant space rockets. If the visitor is lucky there will be a mighty roar with flames as one of the rockets climbs into the sky with a trail of smoke behind it. A blast-off!

The John F. Kennedy Space Center area is the home of American astronauts and the launching spot for rockets, space shuttles, and satellites. At the end of World War II, Americans were studying for an assault on space. The Air Force began operations on Cape Canaveral in 1949 and launched the first rocket in 1950. There were trials and errors but Explorer I, a small satellite, finally went into orbit in 1958. A satellite is in orbit when it is circling the earth in space.

That same year NASA, the National Space Administration, set up a space center at Cape Canaveral. In 1961 Astronaut Alan B. Shepard, Jr., the first space traveller, went 302 miles in fifteen minutes.

Titan III launch at Cape Canaveral

133

President John F. Kennedy was enthusiastic about the space program, aiming at placing a man on the moon. Project Apollo involved a capsule carrying three astronauts in a lunar module. Apollo 11 blasted off on July 16, 1969, and astronaut Neil Armstrong became the first man to set foot on the moon.

One of the astronauts looked back at the earth from the moon. "It was so blue, " he said later, "and so beautiful. All I could think of was they were all fighting down there in that lovely place, Earth." There were successes and disasters in the program. Skylab, a research capsule, was a success when Americans and Russians met in a friendly space rendezvous. The worst disaster was when the Shuttle "Columbia" exploded on takeoff in 1981, killing all seven aboard. One was a school teacher from New Hampshire, Christa McAuliffe.

The Kennedy Space Center continues to send people and missiles into space. Frequent launchings are available for Floridians to watch.

Chapter Thirteen

Artists, Some Florida Originals

The Arts in Florida

Artists are original people who express their thoughts and ideas through special skills. Often artists are called the conscience of society for they tap deep common truths. Some artists are poets, novelists, writers, musicians, composers, conductors. Some are painters, or photographers or sculptors who put thoughts into visual form so others may share their ideas. Some use dance to let the body convey a deep emotion.

Many people who don't possess the special genius for artistic performance support the arts by donating time and money to museums, art education, galleries, and concerts.

Florida's Department of State, Division of Cultural Affairs, and the Florida Arts Council work to have Florida experience art in all its forms. They give grants, information, and encouragement to individuals and local art councils to see that Florida artists are not neglected and that new young artists are recognized. State supported travelling exhibits, concerts, and theater reach most areas of Florida.

Florida ranks high in per capita expenditures for the arts, number eleven nationally in this category. The state appropriation itself is now second in the nation in the amount allocated to the arts.

Florida Arts Council

Florida Arts Council since 1986 has recognized some leading Florida artists by listing them in the Florida Artists Hall of Fame. In 1992 composer and pianist Ray Charles was inducted into the Hall of Fame. Ray Charles was born in Greenville, Florida and after his sight failed, educated in the St. Augustine School for the Deaf and Blind. Well known in the media for his music and his eleven Grammy awards, Charles now lives in California, but Florida is still "home".

Also, in 1992, Duane Hanson of Davie was inducted for his sculpture.

The list of the Hall of Fame includes persons born in Florida and those who have chosen it as home, and is comprised of people who have made significant contributions to arts in Florida, either as donor or performer.

Beginning with the year 1987 those honored are John Ringling, Sarasota, patron and collector; Ernest Hemingway, Key West, writer; Marjorie Kinnon Rawlings, Cross Creek, writer; George Firestone, Miami, patron; Tennessee Williams, Key West, playwright; Zora Neal Hurston, Eatonville, writer and folklorist; John D. Macdonald, Sarasota, writer; and Robert Rauschenberg, Captiva, visual artist.

John and Mabel Ringling

Florida has its own state art museum in Sarasota, a world class collection of paintings by old masters, housed in a magnificent museum. It was a gift from Circus King John Ringling and his wife Mabel. Mabel Ringling shared her husband's tastes and generousity, and together the Ringlings set up one of the world's finest collections of seventeenth century Italian, French, Dutch, and Spanish paintings, tapestries, and sculptures.

To house these treasures they built a stunning gallery in Sarasota, next door to their personal winter palace "Ca'dZan", meaning "House of John". The Ringlings had

no children so they planned this mansion and gallery as
a gift to the people of Florida. Ringling lost money heavily
in the Great Depression, but he never sold any of the
collection which was intended for Florida. The gallery
was first opened to the public in 1930.

After the death of the Ringlings the State of Florida
honored their memory with a circus museum where all
sorts of circus paraphernalia are exihibited including a
collection of circus photographs by photographer Loomis
Dean, a Florida native.

Florida also bought and reconstructed the Asolo Theater, a small nineteenth century building moved piece by
piece from Italy. This theater, the Ringling Art Museum
and Ca'dZan mansion, the Circus Museum and Ringling's
statuary gardens compose Florida's special art center.

The Ringling Museum

Once a multimillionaire, John Ringling had only $311.00 left in his bank account when he died, but he had left "the greatest show on earth" for the future of Florida.

In addition to the Asolo Theater, Florida has performing arts centers in leading cities and exhibition halls in the major universities. Florida supports the Caldwell Theater in Boca Raton, the Hippodrome in Gainesville, and the Coconut Grove Theater in the Miami area.

Zora Neale Hurston

Zora Neale Hurston, author

Hall of Fame writer Zora Neale Hurston was born about 1901 in Eatonville. Being a child of this town in that era gave her special roots, reflected in her novels, essays, and poems.

Eatonville, the setting of her writings, was founded in 1887 by a group of twenty-seven African-American men who had become desperate with discrimination in the post-Civil War days in Florida. They wanted a town where they could live with their own kind, nominate and elect officials and run a town without white interference. With the help of two white philanthrophists from Maitland, who gave them a small piece of land and allowed them to buy more, the town was legally incorporated as Eatonville, as shown in the Orange County records.

A mayor and other town officials were elected. Eatonville has continued as a democratic, all black, town, slowly growing, building houses, churches, businesses. In Zora Neal Hurston's books she describes life in that town where there was no segregation because they were all alike.

Eatonville had its own boarding school, the Hungerford School, established almost as soon as the town itself. Here the black youth of central Florida got a first class education in academics and vocational skills at a time when there were no local high schools for African-Americans. With this unique background many of the Eatonville young people became leaders in the state and country.

Hurston was the daughter of a Baptist minister who was also Eatonville's mayor from 1912 to 1916. After attending the Hungerford School, she went north and ended up with a brilliant academic record at several major universities. She was recognized early as a writer of talent. She studied anthropology at Columbia University and was encouraged to return home to write about her own people, especially their folklore. *Their Eyes Were Watching God,* her novel laid in Eatonville, gives a graphic description of cane workers, floods and hurricanes.

Not only were there more books by her, but about her as well. She was a famous Floridian and American, a friend of eminent writers and poets of her day, part of the 1920's Harlem set. She died poor and all but forgotten in 1960, but her work, probably ahead of its time, is now classic American literature, giving the world a new view of Florida and the souls of women everywhere.

Other Artists

Not all of Florida's artists are listed in the Hall of Fame. Tucked away in small towns or big cities, old and young, artists are plugging away at their own poems, paintings, photographs or other works of art. Everyone must have tried at some time to write a poem in a surge of emotion, but very few succeed in publishing and gaining recognition.

A much published poet is Dr. Edmund Skellings of Dania, who is, in fact, the Poet Laureate of Florida, chosen by the governor and confirmed by the legislature. The Poet Laureate is not paid and has no limited term. Although not a native of Florida, Dr. Skellings has lived, lectured, and read his poems throughout the state for many years. His books are available in most libraries.

Moses Jumper, Jr. another Florida poet, is a Seminole Indian considered the poetic leader of his tribe. He expresses his special thoughts for all Floridians while he works as recreational director for all the Seminole reservations in the state.

Jumper was born and bred in Florida and now lives in Big Cypress. He sees the land with a special inner eye, and he knows that all groups of people need poets to speak for them. He gives us permission to quote a few lines from his book *Echoes in the Wind.*

"Our Native American People are poets,
natural born poets, gifted from within.

Their songs and stories combine the ethics of life, of where we are going and where
we have been."

Audubon

An early painter in Florida, known throughout the world was John James Audubon, whose bird paintings were famous before Florida became a state. Born on a Caribbean island of French parentage, he was educated in France and came to America in 1803 when he was eighteen years old to oversee some of his father's property in Pennsylvania. Left on his own, young Audubon in his personal notes said he cared little for his father's business. "Hunting, fishing, drawing, and music occupied my every moment," he wrote. He also fell in love. Eventually he married Lucy, and with his young family he tried unsuccessfully to become a merchant.

His wife was clever and sympathetic. She realized that her talented husband was meant to be a naturalist and a painter, and she patiently supported the family by teaching while the bankrupt Audubon seriously devoted his entire life to his art, with a burning ambition to publish his own paintings and writings about American birds.

Ornithology, the study of birds, was the rage in the 1800's, and Audubon knew that Florida probably had more birds than any other place in America. By the time that he arrived in St. Augustine in 1831 he was becoming known in Europe and America. For a year he explored and worked in Florida, where he painted over thirty of his famous bird pictures, as far south as the Dry Tortugas.

The Key West house in which he lived while he was painting and sketching is now a memorial museum to Audubon containing a rare volume of his original work.

An Artistic Couple

Two native born Florida artists who are married to each other and who both teach at Florida State University, are Nancy Smith Fichter, Professor of Dance, and Robert W. Fichter, Professor of Art.

When Nancy Smith was a little girl in Jacksonville she read books on ballet and dreamed of being a professional dancer herself. In the 1940's that was not an everyday dream or opportunity, but her summer camp director, author Lillian Smith, encouraged her. At camp she learned about the famous modern dancer Martha Graham.

Later Nancy Smith went to Florida State University (FSU) where there was dance instruction but no dance department. In due time she went to New York to study under Martha Graham herself.

After teaching at FSU for a few years, Smith went to Texas Women's University where she received advanced degrees in dance and related arts.

With the best dance education then available she returned to FSU in 1964 to establish the first dance department.

"I have always choreographed in my mind," she said." My earliest memories are of a commitment to dance as an art form to express thought and feeling."

As Professor of Dance she had free rein with choreography and performance. Today, a Distinguished Professor, famous throughout the dance world, she is a true original who not only teaches and influences Florida men and women, but has gone as far away as Australia and Hong Kong to share her ideas. She writes and lectures as well as teaches. She has originated ninety major choreographic works. Since she is a fifth generation Floridian, it is natural that two of these works are "Wakulla" and "Hamilton County".

Robert W. Fichter is an artist with multiple skills. His modern outlook encompasses a whole new spectrum of communication. He doesn't hesitate to combine photography, acrilics, oil, watercolor, charcoal, etching, crayons, or rubber stamps on one work to put across his ideas, which are original, often political, usually humorous, and a thoughtful reflection of the human race.

As a sixteen year old high school boy in Gainesville he became fascinated with photography and was chosen the art editor of the yearbook. He saw beyond the rows of look-alike photos in the average yearbook and became the high school "avant gardist".

From the start he knew that "a photograph may not look like what we expect." He knew it could be molded in the eyes of an artist. Today as Professor of Art at FSU he exhibits widely, teaching and stimulating art students to new ideas and new forms.

"Artistic expression on paper, canvas, or any surface is possible and fun if you use your skills and discipline", he says. "Show your work and see if the viewer understands. Art is a triangle of the artist's ideas, the work itself, and the response of the viewer."

William P. Foster and His Bands

William P. Foster has brought joy and jazz to Florida. His musical and theatrical genius have led Florida Agricultural and Mechanical University's high stepping musician-dancers to the top of the world's marching bands. Millions of people have seen and heard the "Marching 100" (It now has 250 members) on TV or in stadiums.

His most famous recent performance came to international attention when Foster was asked to bring his band to Paris for the French Bicentennial parade, where 500 million people watched FAMU's finest with their mime, music, dancing, and movement. France had specified that they wanted America's best for their celebration.

When William Foster came to FAMU in 1946 after a solid music education and professional experience, he found sixteen battered instruments but a lot of African-American talent. The late jazz great Julian "Cannonball" Adderly was in Foster's first year's band, and he had the ongoing support of the talented Adderly family, including jazz trumpeter Nat.

Discipline, pride, hard work, and excellence in music come first in the band. Then the movement becomes involved with unique dance forms and rhythms. Cadences range from the slow death march of one step every three seconds to the staccato six steps per second. The music is memorized and the timing must be perfect.

Foster began his musical career at age twelve in Kansas City, Missouri, where he heard, breathed, and absorbed jazz music and motion while he studied classical music. In high school he was the student band conductor. He went on to major in music in college and to get a doctorate in education at Columbia Teachers College. He has directed all the major U.S. service bands and for many years directed the McDonald's All American High School Band.

He writes, composes, teaches, and conducts. He has been selected president of the American Bandmasters Association, the highest award in his field, but he remains "Mr. Music" to the members of his Marching 100.

Coconut Grove, An Artistic Place

A decade after the end of the Civil War south Florida was mostly uninhabited. A few hardy pioneers had built log houses on land grants, and there were Indian trading posts on the Miami River. There was no town until a little jewel of a colony of gentle people began to gather on Biscayne Bay, south of present Miami. This was Coconut Grove.

Ralph Monroe and friends came to Coconut Grove in the 1880's where he set up a boat design and building business. The Peacock family from England built the first public lodging, the Bay View House, which soon became a social and intellectual center. In 1887 Ralph and his friend Kirk Munroe, the writer, established the Biscayne Bay Yacht Club which was another social center.

In Coconut Grove people got around mostly by boat and on foot and built their houses to face the bay. Many of the residents were from New England where they had been influenced by Emerson and Thoreau and liked the simple and natural life. They were intent on preserving the lush tropical environment with its strange flora and fauna.

The little town soon had a library and good schools, a women's club, and churches, and when Flagler wanted to put his railroad into the Grove, the citizens said NO. So the railroad went to Miami instead. Miami, a newer town, had different roots and aims.

Ralph Monroe was a brilliant photographer. He recorded the life and people of this area with his glass negative photographs, many of which are now in the Florida State Archives. His home "The Barnacle" is now a state park, open to visitors who wish to see how life was in the 1880's in the Grove.

Marjorie Stoneman Douglas, whose books have influenced Florida's environmental policies for generations, has lived in Coconut Grove for many years.

To this day, Coconut Grove has managed to keep a sense of identity despite the pushing traffic, runaway growth and tourism. Back on the old streets are descendants of the original Coconut Grovers, including the many black Bahamians and "conchs" from the keys who mingled in the early town. Coconut Grove has always attracted and produced artists. At one time there were more persons per capita listed in "Who's Who" from Coconut Grove than in any other spot in this country.

Chapter Fourteen

Unique Environment; Unique Problems

Hurricanes

A vulnerable finger of land, Florida is hurricane country. Repeated hurricanes have always affected Florida's economic and environmental history. The destructive list is long.

For instance, the colony of Pensacola was wiped out by a hurricane just as it was being established in the sixteenth century. The new city of Miami, already in

Florida hurricane, 1926

economic trouble, was devastated in 1926 when a much publicised hurricane literally blew the town and many inhabitants away. New and better construction laws for a rebuilt town were one good result.

The Lake Okeechobee region was hit by one of the world's worst hurricanes in 1928, flooding the lake and destroying people and the sugar industry. In 1992 Hurricane Andrew demolished Homestead and other farming towns south of Miami with yet unreckoned costs. The list could continue.

Water

Florida, a semi-tropical peninsula with the Atlantic Ocean to the east and the Gulf of Mexico to the west, is unlike any other state. The "detailed tidal shore line", which measures the coast including bays, sounds, and other coastal waters, totals almost 9,000 statute miles. The streams, rivers, and creeks within the state are over 10,000 miles long. There are 882 islands, small and large, in the Florida Keys.

The Gulf Stream, a river in the sea, starts its powerful northward run between Cuba and the Florida Keys and has a substantial southward bound counter current near the shore. These currents move sands and nutrients, and provide a haven for many species of sea life. The Gulf Stream brings warm water to Bermuda, Greenland, Iceland, and the British Isles.

Much of Florida has potable fresh water flowing through strange underground rivers called "aquifers". The same karst geologic formation which provides the aquifers also produces unpredictable sink holes, some with tidal waters which rise and fall with the sea. Karst formations cause lakes that drain without warning and natural bridges where surface streams suddenly go underground, to reappear a short distance away.

There are over 200 springs in Florida, with a combined daily flow of about seven billion gallons of fresh water. In 1971 all public water systems in the state combined to deliver 800 million gallons per day to their customers, or about one ninth of the daily spring flow.

The seas, the sunshine and the winds evaporate sea water into clouds which then pour fresh water onto Florida land in an average annual rainfall of fifty-three inches. Some of this flows back into the sea or recharges aquifers and ground waters.

Lake Okeechobee, Florida's largest lake with an area of 700 square miles, naturally fed water to the Everglades before man-made changes occurred. The wandering Kissimmee River which flows into the lake traditionally watered south and central Florida with its periodic flooding. Recent engineering changed the water system and agricultural situation of this area.

This is a simplified version of complex problems that have developed as Florida land has been more intensively used for food and housing for a growing population.

Efforts to build a cross-Florida canal and reroute the Kissimmee River have been economic failures and environmental disasters according to some experts. Environmentalists feel that such drastic changes might ruin the Florida aquifers, the Everglades, and Lake Okeechobee

The Everglades

The Everglades, described by Marjorie Stoneman Douglas as a "River of Grass", starts at Lake Okeechobee and runs south to Florida Bay, just above the Florida Keys. This is a unique area of about 750 square miles, most of which was originally covered by water in which grasses and other plant life grow. It contains occasional raised areas, limestone reefs in the sea of grass, known as "hammocks", where some trees and tropical plants grow. Indians and others hunt deer and other game on them. A few dry areas produce pine and palmetto growth. The south coast of Florida is covered with unique mangrove forests; unique because the mangrove, unlike most other plants, can live in either fresh or moderately salty marsh water.

Plants and Animals

Papayas, avocados, mangos, key limes, oranges, grapefruit, coconuts and many other exotic fruits are native or have been imported to flourish in Florida. The huge sugar industry, established south of Lake Okeechobee, in about 400,000 acres of the rich soils of the Everglades, produces over one-fifth of the sugar consumed in the United States. Florida has grown from a scattered scrub cattle producer to one of the leading producers of high quality beef cattle. The area between Lake Okeechobee and Kissimmee contains some of the larger cattle ranches in the state. The Homestead area is the vegetable basket of the state.

Everybody associates oranges with Florida, from the Orange Bowl game, to Christmas gift boxes, to Florida names places. Oranges are not a native plant but were introduced by the Spanish explorers into made-to-order climate; they innocently brought "gold" with them. The shining metal gold that explorers came seeking was a vain search, but today the citrus industry, fresh and frozen, is the most important crop in Florida

Protecting Our Environment

Non-renewal resources of the state include quantities of oil and natural gas, phosphates, limestone, sands and gravel. Also included in some of the phosphate mining areas are marketable quantities of uranium.

Rarely seen now is the Florida panther, which is down to only a few dozen animals. This big cat is a variation on the western puma or mountain lion. There are alligators all over the state with occasional crocodiles. The slow, vegetarian, prehistoric relic, the manatee, has been classed as endangered but continues to survive.

The bird life in Florida is so varied and exotic, that

Coastline after global warming

many persons, beginning with Audubon, have been attracted to the state to observe, paint, and photograph these flying residents. The Everglades National Park, established in 1947, contains over one and one-half million acres of land and waters, principally for the protection of the bird life. Ernest F. Coe, of Coconut Grove, is often referred to as the "Father of the Everglades National Park".

In 1905 the Audubon Society began providing funds to pay for four county game wardens in an effort to enforce a new law to protect the plume birds. The demands by well dressed ladies for plume decorated hats, principally from the white egrets and the roseate spoonbill, had created a lucrative market for the slaughter of entire rookeries of these birds by plume hunters.

One of the first wardens employed by the Audubon Society was young Guy Bradley, who resided in Flamingo, and was the son and brother of two men who had been walking mail carriers from Palm Beach to Miami, made famous in Theodore Pratt's book *The Barefoot Mailman*. Guy Bradley was shot and killed in 1905 by a neighbor, a plume hunter, and was found in his boat near Flamingo. He was buried on East Cape where a bronze tablet and an island named Bradley Key are reminders of his dedication to duty. A second game warden, C. G. McLeod was murdered in 1908 near Charlotte Harbor.

People Problems

Problems are generally caused by people, sometimes greedy, sometimes thoughtless, sometimes merely by their presence.

Florida in 1830 had an estimated population of 34,730, most of which was in the northern part of the state. By 1930, the railroads had been built, the roads improved, air travel was beginning to bring people into the state, and the population was 1,468,211. By 1970 the war years of World War II and Korea had passed, and the population had increased to 6,789,443. In 1990 the population was almost thirteen million. It is estimated that, by the year 2000, the population will have increased to about fourteen million.

Each resident of Florida uses about 200 gallons of fresh water every day. With 800 new residents arriving daily, the once bountiful supply of the aquifers is being badly overused. What happens when more water is taken out than drains into the aquifers in a peninsula surrounded by sea water? Simply, the sea water seeps into the water supply, and the resulting ground waters become salty. The soft lawns and tropical plants, the golf courses, swimming pools, and other water consuming elements of the good life in Florida have then made drinking and bathing water scarce or unusable.

Water conservation is the first necessity with efficient faucets, shower heads, and toilets. In the early 1970's, areas in south Florida quietly started injecting treated sewage effluents into the ground, to help prevent salt water intrusion. No tourist industry likes to advertise that visitors may be directly or indirectly drinking sewage, or even tertiary treated sewage, which sanitary engineers describe as potable. Golf courses are sometimes sprayed with treated effluents, including secondary treated waters, which have some nutrients in them.

Some major cities have already gone to expensive dual water systems, which provide potable and bathing water in one system, and flushing, lawn watering and car washing waters in another. Individual homes can separate waste waters, putting water containing human wastes into the sewage system, and gray wash waters into a reusable system.

Energy

Florida's demands for energy, generated by oil, coal, or nuclear reaction have skyrocketed over years of population growth and changing life styles. In old Florida, buildings were constructed with high pitched roofs, overhanging eaves, and cross-ventilation to take advantage of shade and breezes. Ralph Monroe's home, "The Barnacle" in Coconut Grove is a fine example of old tropical construction.

High rise buildings require elevators, and everyone wants air conditioning. Many recent buildings have been constructed with windows that do not open, with fixed glass for vision but not air. Household water is now usually heated by gas or electric heaters, rarely by the solar water heaters once so popular in this land of sunshine.

Chapter Fifteen

Fun and Games-and Money

Visitors

Florida's natural charms attracted people who came to play and make money. After the rails were laid, the hotels and great estates built, the same assets continued to interest nationally known individuals such as one of the world's richest men, Standard Oil's John D. Rockefeller. Rockefeller spent the winters of the last thirteen years of his life in his home "The Casements" in

Tourists at Daytona Beach about 1900

Ormond Beach prior to his death in 1937. He shared his wealth generously with many charities, giving away hundreds of millions of dollars. One of his foundation's projects was research into malaria in Florida. He was also known by many of the children of Florida as the man who shared with them the silver dimes he carried in his pockets on his daily walks.

The inventor Thomas Alva Edison of New Jersey, who was responsible for many items including telegraphic equipment, electric lights, movies, and phonographs had a winter home in Fort Myers until his death in 1931. There is now a museum nearby containing many of his inventions. Henry Ford, who was employed by the Edison Illuminating Company before starting to build, race, and sell autos, and Harvey Firestone, manufacturer of tires, brakes, and spark plugs, also spent winters in Florida. These three gifted men discussed many new ideas with each other, including the possible development of synthetic rubber.

The noted capitalist, yachtsman, and holder of the 1902 land auto speed record of over seventy-six miles per hour, William K. Vanderbilt, had a luxurious winter home on Fisher Island, Miami. This home is now a yacht club for an enclave of nearby private homes.

Alfred I. duPont, explosives manufacturer from Delaware, with his third wife Jessie Ball, maintained a winter home "Epping Forest" at Jacksonville from 1927 until his death in 1935. DuPont, often working through his brother-in-law Edward Ball, made massive investments in Florida, buying in 1926 and 1927 alone some 321,980 acres of north Florida lands plus a railroad, a telephone company, the town of Port St. Joe, and part of the town of Carrabelle. This, along with banks that he controlled, became the foundation for the St. Joe Paper Company and its subsidiaries, which remains one of the state's largest land owners.

In 1946, President Harry Truman, in need of a place to rest and get away from the pressures of the Presidency, decided to use the base commandant's quarters at the Key West Naval Base as his vacation White House. He enjoyed it so much that he made a total of eleven trips, spending 175 days in Key West from then until 1952. The Truman White House has now been restored as a museum. .

Speed: Cars, Boats, Dogs, and Horses

Humans have long tried to get places faster and faster from the early Greek Olympic foot races and the Greek and Roman chariot races to the present time. Once again, Florida's weather, hard Atlantic sand beaches, and long stretches of calm waters appealed to those who were dedicated to speedy travel.

The level and hardpacked sands of Daytona Beach attracted drivers of large, fast automobiles, interested in setting new speed records. As early as 1908, David Bruce-Brown, while still a student at Yale, set a land speed

1924 Boat Races, Miami Beach

record of 109 mph at Daytona Beach. Later the British driver Sir Malcolm Campbell in 1925 and subsequent years established several world records on this beach, both in his special massive car "Bluebird" and in stock cars.

In 1928, young driver Frank Lockhart, while running at about 225 mph, cut a tire on a sea shell and was killed. After this, the large autos began to gradually move from the beaches to the long, level dry lake flats of the deserts of the west. An inland circular race track was built back of Daytona Beach where racing continues to this day. Many records have been established here, including those by a Floridian who attended the University of Florida, "Fireball" Roberts, who raced from 1947 until he was killed at Charlotte, N. C. in 1964 at the age of thirty-five..

While the fast cars were rushing up and down Daytona Beach, boats were being designed and motors produced to cover the water faster and faster. One event which encouraged speed over the water was the Prohibition Act, which was in effect from 1920 until 1933, prohibiting the manufacture or importation of alcoholic beverages. This new law created a speed boat contest between "rum runners" and the law enforcement agencies. The local authorities were assisted after 1923 when the Coast Guard was given the task stopping the smuggling. Florida, with its long coast line and proximity to the Bahamas, where lots of alcohol was available, became the scene of many high speed boat races between law enforcement officers and criminals.

The search for speedier boats and more powerful, faster engines caused some of the best naval architects and engineers to work on new products. In addition to the contests between the law and the rum runners, some individuals were interested in speed records. Two of these were Horace E. Dodge, Jr. an heir of the Dodge auto business, with a winter home in Palm Beach, and Garfield A. "Gar" Wood with a facility in Miami. Both tested their new ideas in Florida waters before they raced in the North and manufactured and sold numerous speed boat "runabouts" to the public.

While the beaches and the waters were being used for speed events, the general spectator public, unable to afford speed boats or race cars, were not left without exposure to speed, usually for gambling purposes. Greyhound and horse racing tracks were built in Florida. A by-product of Florida horse racing has turned out to be the development of lands west of Gainesville and Ocala, where the minerals in soil and water appear to help produce some of the world's finest race horses.

Aviation

Pan American Airways (PAA) base at Dinner Key in Coconut Grove, was a magnet that attracted the attention of well known visitors. Charles Lindbergh, after

Pan American World Airways, Miami's Dinner Key Terminal

flying the first solo flight across the Atlantic in 1927, was employed by PAA as a technical adviser. He stayed in the Miami area as he planned and then flew the developing mail and passenger routes for PAA.

Amelia Earhart, who had flown the Atlantic first as a passenger in 1928, when planning her round-the-world flight in 1937, chose Capt. Fred Noonan, of PAA, a resident of Coconut Grove, as her navigator. Noonan had been PAA's navigator on the first Pacific flights of the "China Clipper". Noonan and Earhart were lost in the Pacific in July 1937 on a flight from Lae, New Guinea to Howland Island, and the mystery of their disappearance has continued to this day.

Movies and Cartoons

Thomas Alva Edison, whose winter home was in Ft. Myers, in 1889 invented and developed one of the first moving picture machines, using a new film developed by George Eastman.

Early movies were made in Jacksonville in 1908, and in other Florida spots where the light and scenery was appropriate to the script, including Coral Gables in 1925. A movie publication in 1915 described Jacksonville and Hollywood as the nation's leading winter production movie centers.

Max Fleisher, an early creator of cartoons, who first combined actual movies with cartoon characters in 1917, maintained a production studio in Miami prior to World War II, competing with Walt Disney of Hollywood. The Disney organization, founded on Hollywood cartoons, later developed Orlando's Disney World attractions in the early 1970's.

Sports

The weather in south and central Florida is made for sports. When the midwinter tourists have returned to northern homes, where better to start practicing, conditioning, and playing the All-American game, baseball?

In 1901 Connie Mack, whose grandson is now a U.S. Senator from Florida, brought his Philadelphia "Athletics" to Jacksonville for spring training. The Brooklyn "Dodgers" followed by coming to St. Augustine in the spring of 1903. Other teams joined them. In the early years, the major league teams, after spring training, slowly travelled north again in their private buses, playing exhibition games with various college and high school teams en route.

Now, there are eighteen major league teams, out of the total of twenty-six, who come to Florida for their spring training. Their practice sessions, plus exhibition games against each other are a great tourist attraction for baseball fans. This activity is also a financial boon for both the teams and Florida's tourist industries.

Walter Lanier "Red" Barber, who lived in Tallahassee until his death in 1992 was a beloved figure in Florida's

Walter Lanier "Red" Barber (R), 1949

baseball history. Red Barber was educated at the University of Florida, and then moved from a job on the university radio station WRUF to an announcing job at WLW, Cincinnati, in 1934. His first assignment was to help report spring training in Tampa for the Cincinnati "Reds", working under their road secretary, "Scotty" Reston, now better known as James Reston, a retired political columnist for the New York Times. Red Barber was an innovator, an outstanding announcer of baseball and other sports and has been recognized by honorary degrees, by being inducted into the national Baseball Hall of Fame in 1978, and named as a Distinguished Alumus of the University of Florida and to membership in the Florida Sports Hall of Fame in 1979.

Football in Florida is important to the state, both financially, and to local pride. There are two National Football League (NFL) professional teams in Florida, the "Miami Dolphins" and the "Tampa Bay Buccaneers". Three Florida universities usually have football teams in the top ten of the nation: the University of Miami, Florida State University, and the University of Florida. All are coached by nationally known coaches. Florida Agricultural and Mechanical University also has a highly competitive football team, plus one of the finest marching bands in the world.

Other Florida sports include basketball, with two professional NBA teams in Orlando and Miami. The Spanish game of *jai alai*, which is played with a hand held racket, a hard ivory ball, against a wall, similar to handball, is played as a gambling sport in about a dozen places from Chattahochee in the panhandle to Miami. Polo, the game of wealthy and skilled horsemen, has long been played in Palm Beach, Lake Worth and Boca Raton.

Wrap-up

From Florida's first people, the prehistoric Indians who crossed the Bering Strait from Asia through North

America to Florida, to the present, a polyglot of humanity has moved into Florida, all seeking something.

The Spanish explorers were seeking gold. The French and British soldiers came to throw the Spanish out. The Americans wanted the land for expansion. Andrew Jackson and his soldiers came to turn the land into a Territory for the United States and to drive the Indians out so the white settlers could get land and safety for families. Black slaves came with the Georgia and Carolina planters who wanted new plantations. (Few Africans came directly to Florida.) Runaway black slaves, escaping from owners in the mid-Atlantic states, came seeking freedom. Seminole Indians, remnants of old tribes, came hoping to reclaim land.

Soldiers, missionaries, traders, adventurers, pirates, idealists came into the no-man's land. Poor people from Appalachia came in oxcarts with hand tools, hoping to find fertile land, fish, fruit, and warm weather for a better life. Railroad builders made it possible for speculators in phosphate, citrus fruit growers, and entrepreneurs of all kinds to come. The rich and the curious, the sick and the old came to inhabit great hotels and new homes.

"Tin can tourists" came in their modest cars to escape the Depression and unemployment in the rest of the country. Hippies came to live out their dreams of a new lifestyle.

People seeking vacation fun came to visit the beaches, the Magic Kingdom at Disneyworld, and major sports events. Cubans and Haitians came for political refuge and a better economy.

They all left their mark, good and bad, including Indian mounds, architectural monuments, great homes and hotels, industries and universities. Thoughtful leaders have governed and tried to solve the problems of people, which is what *Florida's Family Album* is all about.

Appendix I

Comparative Chronology

Date	Florida	North America
300 million to 200 million years ago	Florida is believed to have been covered by chilly seas with whales in the water. Florida's basement begins to grow.	
15,000 to 10,000 years ago	A dry period in the Bering Strait allowed people from Asia to cross into North America. "Paleo", meaning "ancient", Indians spread into Florida. The term "Native American" is confusing, since the newcomers from Asia (or as some believe from Europe as well) were not "indigenous" to this country.	
6,000 to 3,000 years ago	Archaic Indians lived in Florida, descendents of the Paleo people.	
3,000 to 2,000 years ago	Woodland Indian culture developed in Florida, roughly structured into tribes: Timucua, Apalachee, Tocobago, Calusa, and Tequesta. These were the principal people in Florida when the Spanish arrived.	
1,000 years ago	Probably 100,000 Indians lived in Florida.	Vikings from Iceland made explorations and settlements in upper North America.
1492	Christopher Columbus arrived in the Caribbean and claimed America for Spain.	
1513	Juan Ponce de Leon arrived in Florida near present St. Augustine.	
1528	Panfilio de Narvaez arrived near Tampa Bay. Went overland to area of present St. Marks. Built a fleet of rickety ships which soon sank. A few survivors walked to Mexico.	

Date	Florida	North America
1542	*The Journey of Alvar Nunez Cabeza de Vaca* was published in Spain, the account of the survivors of the Narvaez expedition, the first best selling book concerning Florida.	
1539	Hernando de Soto landed at Tampa Bay, walked overland and set up a winter residence at present day Tallahassee. He explored the present southern United States.	English, Dutch,French, and other Europeans began to explore in New England and the Atlantic States.
1559	Tristran de Luna attempted to set up a colony in Pensacola.	
1562	Jean Ribaut, French, entered the St. Johns River.	
1565	Pedro Menendez fought the French. Officially founded St. Augustine.	
1600	Spanish soldiers and missionaries continued to arrive in Florida. The Mission system was constructed. Some Indian outbreaks.	
1607		Jamestown, Virginia, colony founded.
1620	British and French were increasingly interested in Florida.	Pilgrims land at Plymouth, Massachusetts.
1680	A fort and settlement existed at St. Marks.	
1689-1762		French and Indian Wars in New England.
1700	British raids on Spanish settlements.	
1702	5,000 people lived in St. Augustine, including slaves. Piracy and smuggling existed on all Florida coasts.	

Date	Florida	North America
1763	The Treaty of Paris awarded Florida to England.	French and Indian Wars ended in North America.
July 4, 1776	The British flag flew over Florida and Tories were welcomed.	Declaration of Independence signed in Philadelphia.
1775-1783		American Revolution
1784	Spanish rule resumed in Florida. Old Indian tribal names have been superceded by Creeks, Chicasaws, Cherokees, and Miccosukees. Many fewer Indians in Florida. Runaway slaves begin to seek refuge among the Indians.	
1800	Possibly 10,000 people in Florida.	U.S. population is 5,308,483
1808	Inportation of slaves into the United States was stopped.	
1812	Florida was the scene of Spanish and American border disputes.	U. S. declared war on Great Britain.
1814-20	Gen. Andrew Jackson fought Indians, fugitive slaves, and Spanish in the first phase of the Seminole Wars (The Wars of Indian Removal).	
1818	Jackson seized Fort St. Marks and executed two British citizens and two Indian chiefs. Jackson claimed Florida for the U.S.	
1821	Florida formally became a Territory of the U.S. with Andrew Jackson as the Territorial Governor.	
1830	Tallahassee selected as the Capitol of Florida. The railroad age is commencing in the United States. Florida population 34,370	U.S. population 12,860,702

Date	Florida	North America
1832		Samuel Morse invented the telegraph.
1834	Tallahassee-St. Marks Railroad started operations.	
1835	Wars of Indian Removal continue. Osceola imprisoned.	
1838-39	Florida's first Constitutional Convention at St. Joseph.	
1840	Florida Constitution ratified.	
1845	Florida becomes a state. Population 57,951.	
1848	Gold discovered in California.	
1850	Florida population 87,445.	
1851	Dr. John Gorrie of Apalachicola invents artificial ice.	
1858	Seminole Wars end.	
1860	Constitutional Convention at Tallahassee votes $100,000 for Florida troops.	Abraham Lincoln elected President.
1861	Florida secedes from 'Union and joins Confederacy. Over 16,000 troops from Florida serve in war.	Civil War begins.
1862	Lincoln's Emancipation Proclamation frees the slaves only in the Confederate states.	
1864	Confederate troops win the Battles of Olustee and Natural Bridge in Florida.	
1865	Confederacy is defeated. Robert E. Lee surrenders. Slavery ends in the United States. Florida's Governor John Milton commits suicide. Florida suffers under reconstruction.	Lincoln is assassinated.

Date	Florida	North America
1868	Military rule ends in Florida.	
1870	Florida population 187,748	U.S. population 38,558,371.
1898	Spanish-American War	
1900		8,000 autos in U.S.
1908	First motion pictures produced in Florida.	
1914	First scheduled airline, St.Petersburg to Tampa.	
1917-18		World War I
1920	Florida population 968,470.	
1924-25	Florida Land Boom	
1926	Miami hurricane and real estate "bust".	
1928	Lake Okechobee hit by a killer hurricane and flood.	
1929-35		The Great Depression.
1941-45		World War II
1950	Florida population 2,771,305	U.S. population 151,325,798
1961	Space age commences. Astronaut Alan Shepard goes into space from Cape Canaveral, Florida.	President John F. Kennedy assassinated.
1964	Civil Rights Act passed. Florida schools are all integrated by the end of the 1960's.	
1980	Mariel boat lift brings 120,000 Cubans to Florida. 30,000 Haitians also arrive.	
1990	Florida population 12,937,926	U.S. population 248,709.873
1992	Hurricane "Andrew" devastates southern Florida.	

Appendix II

Selected Reading About Florida

Abbey, Kathryn T. *Florida, Land of Change*. Chapel Hill: Univ. of North Carolina Press, 1941.

Arnold, J. Barto III, ed. *Underwater Archaeology Proceedings from the Society for Historical Archaeology Conference*. Baltimore: Society for   Historical Archaeology, 1989.

Barrietos, Bartolome. *Menendez, Pedro de Aviles*. Tr. by Anthony Kerrigan. Gainesville: Univ. of Florida, 1965.

Barrs, Burton. *East Florida in the American Revolution*. Jacksonville: Cooper, 1941.

Bartram, William. *Travels of William Bartram*. Reprint, New Haven: Yale, 1958.

Bowers, Claude. *The Tragic Era*. New York: Houghton Mifflin, 1929.

Brown, Canter, Jr. *Florida's Peace River Frontier*. Orlando: Univ. of Central Florida, 1991.

Bullen, Adelaide K. *Florida Indians of Past and Present*. Gainesville: Univ. of Florida, 1965.

Burnett, Gene M. *Florida's Past*, Vol. I & II. Sarasota: Pineapple, 1986, 1988.

Cabell, Branch and Hanna, A.J. *Rivers of America-The St. Johns, a Parade of Diversities.* New York: Rinehart & Co., 1943.

Cabeza de Vaca, Alvar Nunez. *The Journey of Alvar Nunez Cabeza de Vaca and His Companions from Florida to the Pacific.* Tr. by Fanny Bandelier. New York: Allerton, 1904.

Cabeza de Vaca. *Adventures in the Unknown Interior of America.* Tr. by Cyclone Covey. Albuquerque: Univ. of New Mexico, 1961.

Cash, W. J. *The Mind of the South.* New York: Knopf, 1941.

Cochran, Jacqueline. *The Stars at Noon.* Boston: Atlantic-Little Brown, 1954.

Columbe, Debra, and Hiller, Herbert. *Season of Innocence.* Miami: Pickering, 1988.

Davis, Thomas F. *History of Early Jacksonville, Florida.* Jacksonville: Drew, 1911.

DeMilt, Alonzo. *The Life and Travels of an American Adventurer.* New York: Lovell, 1883.

Didion, Joan. *Miami.* New York: Simon & Schuster, 1987.

Dodd, Dorothy. *Florida Becomes a State.* Tallahassee: Florida Centennial Commission, 1945.

Douglas, Marjorie S. *Florida, the Long Frontier.* New York: Harper & Row, 1967.

Douglas, Marjorie S. *The Everglades, River of Grass.* New York: Rinehart, 1947.

Ellis, Mary Louise and Rogers, William W. *Favored Land Tallahassee.* Norfolk: Donning Co., 1988.

Fairbanks, George. *History and Antiquities of St. Augustine, Florida*. Jacksonville: Drew, 1881.

Fernald, Edward A., Ed. *Atlas of Florida*. Tallahassee: Florida State Univ., 1981.

Gannon, Michael V. *The Cross in the Sand*. Gainesville: Univ. of Florida, 1965.

Giddings, Joshua R. *Exiles of Florida*. Gainesville: Univ. of Florida, Reprint, 1964.

Hanna, A. J. *A Prince in Their Midst*. Norman: Univ. of Oklahoma, 1946.

Harner, Charles E. *Florida's Promoters*. Tampa: Trend House, 1973.

Hoffmeister, John E. *Land From the Sea.* Coral Gables: Univ. of Miami, 1974.

Hopkins, David M. , Ed. *The Bering Land Bridge*. Stanford: Stanford, Univ., 1967.

Hudson, Charles. *The Southeastern Indians*. Knoxville: Univ. of Tennessee , 1976.

Ingalls, Robert P., Ed. *Tampa Bay History, A Centennial History of Ybor City*. Tampa: Univ. of South Florida, 1985.

Jahoda, Gloria. *Florida, A Bicentennial History*. New York: Norton, 1976.

Jahoda, Gloria. *The Other Florida*. New York: Scribners, 1967.

Kendrick, Bayard. *Florida Trails to Turnpikes 1914, 1964*. Gainesville: Univ. of Florida, 1964.

Kennedy, Stetson. *The Klan Unmasked*. Boca Raton: Florida Atlantic Univ., 1990 (reprint).

Kennedy, Stetson. *Palmetto Country*. Tallahassee: Florida A&M Univ., 1989.

Milanich, Jerald T. and Fairbanks, Charles H. *Florida Archaeology*. Orlando: Academic, 1980.

Morris, Allen. *The Florida Handbook*. Biennial Series. Tallahassee: Peninsular, 1947-1992.

Mowatt, Chas. L. *East Florida as a British Province*. Berkeley: Univ. of Calif.,1943.

Mudd, Nettie. *The Life of Dr. Samuel Mudd*. Marietta, Ga.: Continental, 1955.

Muir, Helen. *Miami, U.S.A.* New York: Holt, 1953.

Murphy, Jim. *The Boys War*. New York: Scholastic, Inc., 1991.

McGovern, James R., Ed. *Andrew Jackson and Pensacola*. Pensacola: Bicentennial Series, 1974.

Neyland, Leedell. *Twelve Black Floridians*. Tallahassee: Florida A&M Foundation, 1970.

Nulty, William H. *Confederate Florida*. Tuscaloosa: Univ. of Alabama, 1990.

Owsley, Frank L. Jr. *The C.S.S. Florida*. Tuscaloosa: Univ. of Alabama, 1987.

Paisley, Clifton. *The Red Hills of Florida*. Tuscaloosa: Univ. of Alabama, 1989.

Parks, Arva Moore. *The Forgotten Frontier*. Miami: Banyan, 1980.

Patrick, Rembert W. *Florida Under Five Flags*. Gainesville: Univ. of Florida, 1945.

Proby, Kathryn H. *Audubon in Florida*. Coral Gables: Univ. of Miami, 1974.

Rawlings, Marjorie K. *Cross Creek*. New York: Scribners, 1942.

Scott, John I. *The Education of Black People in Florida*. Philadelphia: Dorrance, 1974.

Shofner, Jerrell H. *Jefferson County, Florida*. Tallahassee: Sentry, 1976.

Shofner, Jerrell H. *Daniel Ladd-Merchant Prince of Florida*. Gainesville: Univ. of Florida, 1978.

Silverberg, Robert. *The Mound Builders*. Athens: Ohio Univ., 1986.

Swanton, John R. *Final Report of the U.S. de Soto Expedition Commission*. Washington: Smithsonian, 1985.

Tebeau, Charlton W. *Man in the Everglades*. Coral Gables: Univ. of Miami, 1968.

Tebeau, Charlton W. *A History of Florida*. Miami: Univ. of Miami, 1971.

Walthall, John A. *Prehistoric Indians of the Southeast*. Tuscaloosa: Univ. of Alabama, 1980.

Wickman, Patricia. *Osceola's Legacy*. Tuscaloosa: Univ. of Alabama, 1991.

Weisman, Brent R. *Like Beads on a String*. Tuscaloosa: Univ. of Alabama, 1989.

Williams, John Lee. *Territory of Florida*. (1837 fac. ed.) Gainesville: Univ. of Florida, 1962.

All issues of *The Florida Historical Quarterly*. Tampa: The Florida Historical Society.

Some Fiction About Florida for All Ages

Benet, Stephen Vincent. *Spanish Bayonet*. New York: George H. Doran Co., 1926.

Cheney, Cora. *Key of Gold*. New York: Henry Holt, 1955.

Cheney, Cora. *The Rocking Chair Buck*. New York: Henry Holt, 1956.

Hurston, Zora N. *Their Eyes Were Watching God*. Philadelphia: Lippincott, 1937.

Matthiessen, Peter. *Killing Mr. Watson*. New York: Random House, 1991.

Rawlings, Marjorie K. *The Yearling*. New York: Scribners, 1938.

Appendix III

Some Facts About Florida

Earliest known human settlement: by Paleo Indians from Asia, about 10,000 to 15,000 years ago.

First known European contact: Spanish explorer Juan Ponce de Leon, 1513.

After Spanish, French and British periods, became a Territory of the United States in 1821.

Admitted to Union as a State: 1845. Capitol: Tallahassee.

Seceded from Union and joined the Confederate States of America: 1861.

Restored to Union: 1868.

Some Geography:

Total area, land and water: 58,560 square miles.

Coast line, Atlantic and Gulf of Mexico: 1,146 miles.

No point in the state is more than 60 miles from sea water.

Length, St. Mary's River to Key West: 447 miles.

Width, Atlantic Ocean to Perdido River: 361 miles.

Highest natural land altitude: 345 feet, Walton County.

Number of Counties: 67

State Symbols:

State bird: Mockingbird.

State flower: Orange Blossom.

State tree: Sabal palm.

State song: Old Folks at Home

State nickname: The Sunshine State

Resident's nickname: Florida Cracker, which originated from Florida cowboys cracking their cattle whips.

Appendix IV

Governors of Florida

Territorial
Andrew Jackson, East and West Florida, 1821.

William G. D. Worthington,
Acting, East Florida, 1821-1822.

Col. George Walton, Acting, West Florida, 1821-1822.

William P. DuVal, 1822-1834.

John H. Eaton, 1834-1835.

Richard Keith Call, 1835-1840.

Robert Raymond Reid, 1840-1841.

Richard Keith Call, 1841-1844.

John Branch, 1844-1845.

State
William D. Moseley, 1845-1849.

Thomas Brown, 1849-1853.

James E, Broome, 1853-1857.

Madison S. Perry, 1857-1861.

John Milton, (Confederate State), 1861-1865.

A.K. Allison, Acting, 1865.

William Marvin, Provisional, 1865.

David S. Walker, 1865-1868.

Harrison Reed, 1868-1872.

Ossian B. Hart, 1873-1874.

M.L. Stearns, 1874-1877.

George F. Drew, 1877-1881.

William D. Bloxham, 1881-1885.

Edward A. Perry, 1885-1889.

Francis P. Fleming, 1889-1893.

Henry L. Mitchell, 1893-1897.

William D. Bloxham, 1897-1901.

William S. Jennings, 1901-1905.

Napoleon B. Broward, 1905-1909.

Albert W. Gilchrist, 1909-1913.

Park Trammel, 1913-1917.

Sidney J. Catts, 1917-1921.

Cary A. Hardee, 1921-1925.

John W. Martin, 1925-1929.

Doyle E. Carlton, 1929-1933.

David Sholtz, 1933-1937.

Fred P. Cone, 1937-1941.

Spessard L. Holland, 1941-1945.

Millard F. Caldwell, 1945-1949.

Fuller Warren, 1949-1953.

Dan T. McCarty, 1953.

Charley E. Johns, 1953-1955.

LeRoy Collins, 1955-1961.

Farris Bryant, 1961-1965.

Haydon Burns, 1965-1967.

Claude R. Kirk, Jr., 1967-1971.

Reubin O'D. Askew, 1971-1979.

D. Robert Graham, 1979-1987.

Wayne Mixon, 1987.

Robert Martinez, 1987-1991.

Lawton Chiles, 1991.

INDEX

ABOUT THE AUTHORS

Ben Partridge (CAPT. USN [Ret]) is a fifth generation Floridian whose people came into Jefferson and Leon Counties in the 1820's. His great grandfather was a delegate to the First Florida Constitutional Convention of 1838-39. His undergraduate work was at the University of Florida and graduate work at The American University in Washington and the University of Miami (Fla) Law School. After retirement from the Navy he did environmental and resource development legal work in several states.

Cora Cheney is the author of 23 children's books, several co-authored with her husband Ben Partridge, and was a long time newspaper reporter and columnist. She attended Florida State College for Women (now FSU) where she studied history under Dr. Kathryn Abbey. Later she graduated in journalism from the University of Georgia, received an MEd. from Antioch, and a MA in Theology from Episcopal Divinity School. She is a retired Episcopal priest. The Partridges have lived in many parts of Florida and in much of the rest of the world and now live in historic St. Marks on the Wakulla River.